FABULOU FLOWERS FOR THE HOME

FABULOUS FLOWERS FOR THE HOME

FIFTY INSPIRATIONAL PROJECTS FOR CONTEMPORARY FLORAL DESIGNERS

FIONA BARNETT
PHOTOGRAPHS BY DEBBIE PATTERSON

HERMES
HOUSE

THIS EDITION IS PUBLISHED BY HERMES HOUSE

HERMES HOUSE IS AN IMPRINT OF ANNESS PUBLISHING LTD
HERMES HOUSE, 88–89 BLACKFRIARS ROAD, LONDON SE1 8HA
TEL. 020 7401 2077; FAX 020 7633 9499; INFO@ANNESS.COM

© ANNESS PUBLISHING LTD 1996, 2003

A CIP CATALOGUE RECORD FOR THIS BOOK IS AVAILABLE FROM THE BRITISH LIBRARY.

PUBLISHER: JOANNA LORENZ
TEXT: FIONA BARNETT AND ROGER EGERICKX
DESIGNER: NIGEL PARTRIDGE
PHOTOGRAPHER: DEBBIE PATTERSON

Previously published as *New Ways With Fresh Flowers*

1 3 5 7 9 10 8 6 4 2

CONTENTS

· · ·

INTRODUCTION

From an intricate corsage to a simple tied posy,
flower arranging requires care and consideration.
In the following pages advice is given on colour,
balance, scale and proportion, flower care, equipment, containers and using fruit and vegetables in
displays. Wiring techniques are also fully
explained, thereby enabling the reader to create
beautiful flower displays with confidence.

Right: These tulips create a wonderful domed effect which can be viewed from any side.

Below: The red dogwood form a decorative structure to this arrangement.

Below: A wedding bouquet must be in scale with the person carrying it.

BALANCE

Balance is very important in a flower display, both physically and visually. Foremost, the flower arranger must ensure the physical stability of the display. This involves understanding the mechanics of the arrangement, the types and sizes of materials used, how they are positioned and in what type of container. Different types of floral displays require different strategies to ensure their stability.

A large arrangement to be mounted on a pedestal will need a heavy, stable container. The display materials should be distributed evenly around the container and the weight concentrated as near the bottom as possible. Make sure the longer flowers and foliage do not cause the display to become top-heavy.

A mantelpiece arrangement can be particularly difficult to stabilise since the display materials hanging down over the shelf will tend to pull it forward. So use a heavy container and position the flowers and foliage as far back in it as possible.

Check the stability of an arrangement at regular stages during its construction.

Achieving a visual balance in a flower arrangement involves scale, proportion and colour as well as creating a focal point in the display.

The focal point of an arrangement is an area to which the eye should be naturally drawn and from which all display materials should appear to flow. While the position of the focal point will vary according to the type of display, generally speaking it will be towards its centre. This is where the boldest colours and shapes should be concentrated, with paler colours around the outside.

Always think of the display in three dimensions, never forgetting that as well as a front, it will have sides and a back. This is not difficult to remember for a bouquet or a free-standing, pedestal-mounted display, but can be forgotten if a display is set against a wall. Even a flat-backed arrangement needs depth and shape. Recessing materials around the focal point will help give it depth and weight.

Balance in a floral display is the integration of all visual factors to create a harmonious appearance and with practice you will develop the ability to achieve this.

SCALE AND PROPORTION

Scale is a very important consideration when planning a floral display.

In order to create an arrangement which is pleasing to the eye, the sizes of different flower types used in the same display should not be radically different. For example, it would be difficult to make amaryllis look in scale with lily-of-the-valley.

The type of foliage used should be in scale with the flowers, the display itself must be in scale with its container, and the arrangement and its container must be in scale with its surroundings. A display in a large space in a public building must itself be appropriately large enough to make a statement, conversely a bedside table would require no more than an arrangement in a bud vase.

Proportion is the relationship of width, height and depth within a floral display and in this respect there are some rule-of-thumb guidelines worth bearing in mind.
❖ In a tied bouquet, the length of the stems below the binding point should be approximately one-third of the bouquet's overall height.

❖ In a trailing wedding bouquet, the focal point of the display will probably be about one-third of the overall length up from its lowest point.

❖ For a pedestal arrangement, the focal point will be approximately two-thirds of the overall height down from its topmost point.

❖ A vase with long-stemmed flowers such as lilies, should be around one-third the height of the flowers.

❖ The focal point of a corsage is about one-third the overall height up from the bottom.

However, remember that decisions on the scale and proportion of a floral display are a matter of personal taste and thus will vary from person to person.

The important thing is not simply to accept a series of rules on scale and proportion but to give these factors your consideration and develop your own critical faculties in this area.

COLOUR

The way in which colour is used can be vital to the success or failure of a display and there are several factors to bear in mind when deciding on a colour palette.

Though most people have an eye for colour, an understanding of the theory of colour is useful. Red, blue and yellow are the basic hues from which all other colours stem. Red, orange and yellow are warm colours which tend to create an exciting visual effect, while green, blue and violet are cooler and visually calmer.

Generally speaking, the lighter, brighter and hotter a colour, the more it will dominate an arrangement. White (which technically is the absence of colour) is also prominent in a display of flowers.

On the other hand, the darker and cooler the colour, the more it will visually recede into a display. It is important to bear this in mind when creating large displays to be viewed from a distance. In such circumstances blue and violet, in particular, can become lost in an arrangement.

Usually a satisfactory visual balance should be achieved if the stronger, bolder coloured flowers are positioned towards the centre of the display with the paler, more subtle colours around the outside.

Now armed with some basic knowledge of colour theory you can be braver in your choice of palette. "Safe" colour combinations such as creams with whites, or pinks with mauves have their place, but experiment with oranges and violets, yellows and blues, even pinks and yellows and you will add a vibrant dimension to your flower arranging.

Above: A contorted branch makes an unusual "trunk" for this cabbage topiary tree.

Top left: The heavy blossoms of white lilac are set against the darker stems of pussy willow and cherry.

Above: These bright yellow sunflowers are complemented by the brown contorted hazel twigs.

Left: The natural greens, yellows and mauves of these herbs blend perfectly together.

9

CONTAINERS

· · ·

While an enormous range of suitable, practical, purpose-made containers is available to the flower arranger, with a little imagination alternatives will present themselves, often in the form of objects we might not have at first glance expected. An old jug or teapot, a pretty mug that has lost its handle, an unusual-looking tin, a bucket, a jam jar, all these offer the arranger interesting opportunities.

Remember, if the container is for fresh flowers, it must be watertight or properly lined. Consider the scale and proportion of the container both to the particular flowers you are going to use, and the type of arrangement.

Do not forget the container can be a hidden part of the design, simply there to hold the arrangement, or it can be an integral and important feature in the overall arrangement.

BAKING TINS (PANS)
Apart from the usual round, square or rectangular baking tins (pans), a number of novelty shapes are available. Star, heart, club, spade and diamond shaped baking tins (pans) are used to make cakes that are out of the ordinary and they can also be used very effectively to produce interesting flower arrangements.

These tins (pans) are particularly good for massed designs, either of fresh or dried flowers, but remember, the tin may need lining if it is being used for fresh flowers.

BASKETS
Baskets made from natural materials are an obvious choice for country-style, informal displays. However, there is a wide range of basket designs available to suit many different styles.

Large baskets are good for table or static displays while smaller baskets

This simple vase perfectly complements the sculptural impact of the arum lilies.

with handles can be carried by bridesmaids or filled with flowers or plants and made into lovely gifts. Traditional wicker baskets can be obtained which incorporate herbs or lavender in their weave.

Wire or metal baskets offer an ornate alternative to wicker and twig, since the wire can be formed into intricate shapes and also can have a more modern look.

CAST-IRON URNS
More expensive than many other types of container, the investment in a cast-iron urn is repaid by the splendid classic setting it offers for the display of flowers. Whether the arrangement is large and flowing or contemporary and linear, the visual strength of a classical urn shape will provide the necessary underpinning.

Of course the physical weight of a cast-iron urn is a factor to consider; it is a plus in that it will remain stable with the largest of displays but a minus when it comes to moving it!

ENAMELLED CONTAINERS
The appeal of using an enamelled container probably lies in the bright colours available. Containers in strong primary colours work well with similarly brightly coloured flowers to produce vibrant displays.

GALVANIZED METAL BUCKET AND POT
The obvious practical advantage of galvanized metal containers is that they will not rust. The attractive silvered and polished texture is ideal for contemporary displays in both fresh and dried flowers.

Today lots of shapes and sizes of containers are available with a galvanized finish but even an old-fashioned bucket can be used to good effect in flower arranging.

GLASS VASES
A glass vase is often the first thing that springs to mind for flower arranging. And indeed, there is an enormous range of purpose-made vases available.

The proportions of this design give prominence to the classical urn.

Particularly interesting to the serious flower arranger will be simple clear glass vases which are made in all the sizes and geometric shapes you could ever need. Their value lies in their lack of embellishment which allows the arrangement to speak for itself. Remember the clear glass requires that the water be changed regularly and kept scrupulously clean, since below the water is also part of the display.

There are also many other forms of vase – frosted, coloured, textured, and cut glass – and all have their place in the flower arranger's armoury.

PITCHERS

Pitchers of all types are ideal flower receptacles. Ceramic, glass, enamelled or galvanized metal; short, tall, thin, fat – whatever their shape, size or colour, they offer the flower arranger a wide range of options.

Displays can range from the rustic and informal to the grand and extravagant, depending on your choice of pitcher and materials.

A varied selection from the vast range of containers that can by used for flower arranging.

PRE-FORMED PLASTIC FOAM SHAPES

Clean to handle, convenient to use, pre-formed plastic foam comes in a wide range of shapes and sizes such as circles, crosses, rectangles and even "novelty" designs like stars, numerals, hearts and teddy bears. Each shape is a moisture-retaining foam with a watertight backing. Equivalent foam shapes are available for dried flowers.

Although often associated with funeral and sympathy designs, pre-formed plastic foam shapes also offer the flower arranger a variety of bases for many other types of display.

TERRACOTTA PLANT POTS

Traditional or modern, the terracotta pot can be utilized to hold an arrangement of flowers and not just plants. If the arrangement is built in plastic foam, line the pot with cellophane (plastic wrap) before

inserting the foam, to prevent leakage. Alternatively just pop a jam jar or bowl into the pot to hold the water.

The appearance of terracotta pots can be changed very effectively by techniques such as rubbing them with different coloured chalks, or treating them with gold leaf. They can also be aged by the application of organic materials such as sour milk which, if left, will enable a surface growth to develop.

WOODEN TRUGS AND BOXES

Old-fashioned wooden trugs and seedboxes can make charming and effective containers for floral displays. Their rustic appeal makes them particularly suitable for informal country-style designs where the container is an enhancing feature. Rubbing the surface of a wooden container with coloured chalk can create an entirely new look.

Of course you must remember to line the box with waterproof material if fresh flowers or plants are going to be used in the display.

EQUIPMENT

· · ·

The flower arranger can get by with the minimum of equipment when he or she is just starting out. However, as he or she becomes more adventurous, a selection of specialized tools and equipment will be useful. This section itemizes those pieces of equipment used in the projects contained in the book.

CELLOPHANE (PLASTIC WRAP)

As wrapping for a bouquet, cellophane (plastic wrap) can transform a bunch of flowers into a lovely gift, and it has a more practical use as a waterproof lining for containers. Also, it can look very effective scrunched up in a vase of water to support flower stems.

FLORIST'S ADHESIVE

This very sticky glue is supplied in a pot and is the forerunner to the hot, melted adhesive of the glue gun. It is necessary when attaching synthetic ribbons or other materials which might be adversely affected by the heat of a glue gun.

FLORIST'S ADHESIVE TAPE

This is a strong adhesive tape used to secure plastic foam in containers. Although it will stick under most circumstances, avoid getting it too wet as this will limit its adhesive capability.

PLASTIC FOAM

Plastic foam comes in a vast range of shapes, sizes and densities, and is available for both dry and fresh flowers. While the rectangular brick is the most familiar, other shapes are available for specific purposes.

Plastic foam is lightweight, convenient to handle and very easy to cut and shape with just a knife. A brick of plastic foam for fresh flowers soaks up water very quickly

Before starting to build a design make sure you have all the materials close to hand.

(approximately 1½ minutes) but must not be resoaked as the structure alters and its effectiveness will be reduced. Plastic foam for dried flowers can seem too hard for the delicate stems of some flowers but a softer version is available, so consider which type you need before starting the design.

FLORIST'S SCISSORS

A strong, sharp pair of scissors are the flower arranger's most important tool. As well as cutting all those things you would expect, the scissors must also be sturdy enough to cut woody stems and even wires.

FLORIST'S TAPE (STEM-WRAP TAPE)

This tape is not adhesive, but the heat of your hands will help secure it to itself as it is wrapped around a stem

The tape is used to conceal wires and seal stem ends. It is made either from plastic or crêpe paper and it will stretch to provide a thin covering. The tape is available in a range of colours although green is normally used on fresh flowers.

FLORIST'S WIRE

Wire is used to support, control and secure materials, also to extend stems and to replace them where weight reduction is required. The wire tends

to be sold in different lengths. Most of the projects in this book use 36 cm (14 in) lengths. Always use the lightest gauge of wire you can while still providing sufficient support. The most popular gauges are:

1.25mm (18g)	0.28mm (31g)
0.90mm (20g)	0.24mm (32g)
0.71mm (22g)	Silver reel
0.56mm (24g)	*(rose) wires:*
0.46mm (26g)	0.56mm (24g)
0.38mm (28g)	0.32mm (30g)
0.32mm (30g)	0.28mm (32g)

Make sure that the wires are kept in a dry place because any moisture will cause them to rust.

GLOVES

While some flower arranging processes would be impeded by gloves, it makes sense to protect your hands whenever necessary, especially if handling materials with sharp thorns or sap which might irritate the skin. So keep some domestic rubber gloves and heavy-duty gardening gloves in your florist's workbox.

GLUE GUN

The glue gun is an electrically powered device fed by sticks of glue, which it melts to enable the user to apply glue via a trigger action. In floristry it is a relatively recent development but invaluable in allowing the arranger to attach dried or fresh materials to swags, garlands or circlets securely, cleanly and efficiently.

The glue and the tip of the gun are extremely hot, so take care at all times when using a glue gun. Never leave a hot glue gun unattended.

PAPER RIBBON

Paper ribbon is an alternative to satin and synthetic ribbon and is available in a large range of mostly muted, soft

colours. It is sold twisted and rolled up. Cut the length of ribbon required in its twisted state and carefully untwist and flatten it to its full width before creating your bow.

PINHOLDER

The pinholder is a heavy metal disc approximately 2 cm (¾ in) thick which has an even covering of sharp metal pins, approximately 3 cm (1¼ in) long. Pinholders are available in a range of diameter sizes for different displays.

The pinholder is placed under the water and the bottom of the flower stems are pushed on to the pins. The weight of the stems is balanced by the weight of the pinholder. It is ideal for creating *Ikebana*-style displays or twiggy linear arrangements.

RAFFIA

A natural alternative to string and ribbon, raffia has several uses for the flower arranger. It can be used, a few strands at a time, to tie together a hand-arranged, spiralled bunch, or to attach bunches of dried or fresh

Start with the basic equipment and add items as your skill develops.

flowers to garlands and swags. In thicker swathes it can also be used to finish bouquets and arrangements by tying them off and being formed into decorative bows.

ROSE STRIPPER

This ingenious little device is a must when handling very thorny roses. Squeeze the metal claws together and pull the stripper along the stem, and the thorns and leaves will be removed. There is also a blade attachment to cut stem ends at an angle. Always wear thick gardening gloves.

SATIN RIBBON

Available in a large variety of widths and colours, satin ribbon is invaluable to the flower arranger when a celebratory final touch is required.

Satin ribbon is preferable to synthetic ribbon because it looks and feels so much softer. Its only drawback is that it frays when cut.

SECATEURS (GARDEN CLIPPERS)

These are necessary to cut the tougher, thicker stems and branches of foliage. Always handle scissors and secateurs with care and do not leave within the reach of young children.

TWINE

String or twine is essential when tying spiralled bunches, making garlands or attaching foliage to gates and posts.

WIRE MESH

Although plastic foam now offers much more flexibility for the flower arranger, wire mesh still has its place in the florist's armoury.

When creating large displays, wire mesh is essential to strengthen the plastic foam and prevent it from crumbling when large numbers of stems are pushed into it. The mesh should be cut in lengths from the roll, crumpled slightly, laid over the top and wrapped around the sides of the foam and wedged between it and the container, then secured in place with florist's adhesive tape.

13

TECHNIQUES

· · ·

TAPING

Stems and wires are covered with florist's tape (stem-wrap tape) for three reasons: first, cut materials which have been wired can no longer take up water and covering with tape seals in the moisture that already exists in the plant; second, the tape conceals the wires, which are essentially utilitarian, and gives a more natural appearance to the false stem; third, wired dried materials are covered with florist's tape (stem-wrap tape) to ensure that the material does not slip out of the wired mount.

1 Hold the wired stem near its top with the end of a length of florist's tape (stem-wrap tape) between the thumb and index finger of one hand. With your free hand, hold the remainder of the length of tape at 45° to the wired stem, keeping it taut. Starting at the top of the stem, just above the wires, rotate the flower slowly to wrap the tape around both the stem and wires, working down. By keeping it taut, the tape will stretch into a thin layer around the stem and wires. Each layer should overlap and stick to the one before. If so desired, you may add flowerheads at different heights as you tape to create units. Finally, fasten off just above the end of the wires by squeezing the tape against itself to stick it securely.

MAKING A STAY WIRE

1 Group together four .71 wires, each overlapping the next by about 3 cm (1¼ in). Start taping the wires together from one end using florist's tape (stem-wrap tape). As the tape reaches the end of the first wire add another .71 wire to the remaining three ends of wire and continue taping, and so on, adding wires and taping four together until you achieve the required length of stay wire.

SINGLE LEG MOUNT

This is for wiring flowers which have a strong natural stem or where a double weight of wire is not necessary to support the material.

1 Hold the flowers or foliage between the thumb and index finger of one hand while taking the weight of the material (i.e. the flowerheads) cross the top of your hand. Position a wire of the appropriate weight and length behind

the stem about one-third up from the bottom. Bend the wire ends together with one leg shorter than the other. Holding the short wire leg parallel with the stem, wrap the long wire leg firmly around both the stem and the other wire leg three or four times. Straighten the long wire leg to extend the stem. Cover the stem and wire with florist's tape (stem-wrap tape).

DOUBLE LEG MOUNT

This is formed in the same way as the single leg mount but extends the stem with two equal length wire legs.

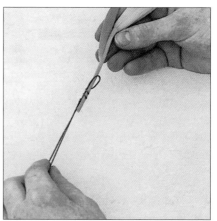

1 Hold the flower or foliage between the thumb and index finger of one hand while taking the weight of the plant material (i.e. the flowerheads) across the top of your hand. Position a wire of appropriate weight and length behind the stem about one-third of the way up from the bottom. One-third of the wire should be to one side of the stem with two-thirds to the other. Bend the wire parallel to the stem. One leg should now be about twice as long as the other.

Holding the shorter leg against the stem, wrap the longer leg around both stem and the other wire to secure. Straighten both legs which should now be of equal length.

PIPPING

Pipping is the process whereby small flowerheads are removed from a main stem to be wired individually. This process can be used for intricate work with small delicate plant materials.

1 Bend a thin silver wire into a hairpin about its centre and twist at the bend to form a small loop above the two projecting legs.

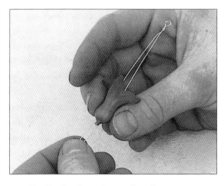

2 Push the legs into the flower centre, down through its throat, and out of its base to create a stem.

3 Using more silver wire, double leg mount this stem with any natural existing stem, and tape if required.

UNITS

A unit is the composite stem formed from two or more pieces of plant material. Units of small flowers can be used in corsages and hair-comb decorations, and units of larger flowers in wired wedding bouquets.

Units should be made up of one type of material only. For small units, first wire and tape the individual flowerheads, buds or leaves.

1 Start with the smallest of the plant material and attach a slightly larger head to it by taping the wires together. Position the larger head in line with the bottom of the first item. Increase the size of the items as you work downward.

For units of larger flowers you may have to join the wire stems by double leg mounting them with an appropriate weight of wire before taping.

EXTENDING THE LENGTH OF A STEM

Flowerheads with short stems, and flowers that are delicate may need the extra support of an extended stem. There are two methods of extending a stem.

1 Wire the flowerhead using the appropriate method and correct

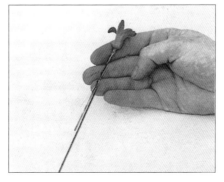

weight of wire. Then single leg mount the wired flowerhead using a .71 wire and tape the wires and any natural stem with florist's tape (stem-wrap tape).

Alternatively, push a .71 wire into the base of the flowerhead from the bottom, then at right angles to this push through a .38 silver wire from one side to the other.

Bend the .38 silver wire so that the two ends point downwards, parallel to the .71 wire. Wrap one leg of .38 wire firmly around its other leg and the .71 wire. Cover with florist's tape (stem-wrap tape).

WIRING AN OPEN FLOWERHEAD

This is a technique for the wiring of individual heads of lily, amaryllis and tulip and is also suitable for small, soft or hollow-stemmed flowers such as anemones and ranunculus.

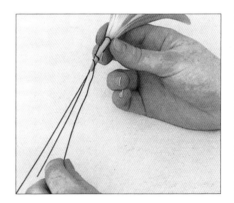

1 Cut the stem of the flower to around 4 cm (1½ in). Push one .71 wire up through the inside of the stem and into the base of the flowerhead. Double leg mount the stem and its internal wire with a .71 wire. Tape the stem and wire.

The internal wire will add strength to the flower's natural stem and the double leg mount will ensure that the weight of the flowerhead is given sufficient support.

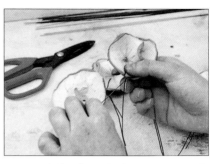

Preserved (dried) apple slices require careful handling when wiring.

WIRING A ROSE HEAD

Roses have relatively thick, woody stems so to make them suitable for use in intricate work, such as buttonholes, headdresses and corsages, the natural stem will need to be replaced with a wire stem.

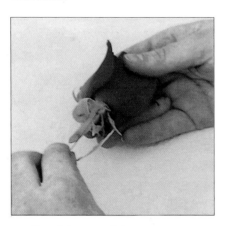

1 Cut the stem of the rose to a length of about 3 cm (1¼ in).
Push one end of a .71 wire through the seed box of the rose at the side. Holding the head of the rose very carefully in your hand (as it is very fragile), wrap the wire several times firmly around and down the stem. Straighten the remaining wire to extend the natural stem. Cover the wire and stem with florist's tape (stem-wrap tape).

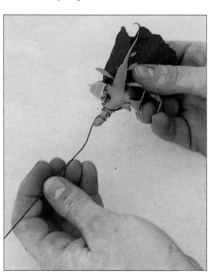

WIRING FRUIT AND VEGETABLES

Using fruit and vegetables in swags, wreaths and garlands, or securing them in plastic foam displays will require wiring them first. The method will depend on the item to be wired and how it is to be used.

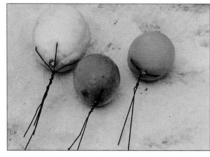

Heavy fruits and vegetables, such as oranges, lemons or bulbs of garlic, will need a heavy .71 wire or even .90. The wire should be pushed through the item, just above its base from one side to the other. Push another wire through the item at right angles to the first and bend all four projecting wires to point downwards.

1 Depending on how the fruit or vegetables will be used, either cut the wires to a suitable length to be pushed into plastic foam, or twist the wires together to form a single stem.

2 Small delicate fruits and vegetables such as mushrooms or figs need careful handling as their flesh is easily damaged. They normally only need one wire. Push the wire through the

base of the item from one side to the other and bend the two projecting wires downwards. Depending on how the material is to be used, either twist to form a single stem, or trim to push into plastic foam.

For the soft materials .71 is the heaviest weight of wire you will require. In some instances, fruit or vegetables can be attached or secured in an arrangement by pushing a long wire "hairpin" right through the item and into the plastic foam behind.

3 Fruit or vegetables that have a stem, such as bunches of grapes or artichokes, can be double leg mounted on their stems with appropriate weight wires.

Extend the length of a starfish by double leg mounting one of its legs.

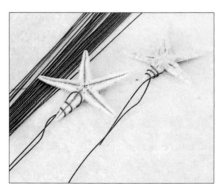

FRUIT AND VEGETABLES IN FLOWER DISPLAYS

The colours and textures of fruit and vegetables can provide harmony or contrast to enhance flower arrangements. The acid colours of citrus fruits, and autumn tints of apples and pears are all readily available to the flower arranger.

Some fruits such as pomegranates, passion fruits and blood oranges are particularly attractive when they have

The strong forms of fruit and vegetables lend themselves well to displays such as this wall swag (above) and unusual obelisk (right). Careful wiring ensures the materials stay in position.

been cut or torn open to reveal their flesh. However, remember that open fruits will deteriorate quickly so only use them for short-term displays at special events, parties or dinners.

Vegetables might seem a surprising choice for use in flower arrangements but the subtle colours and textures can be combined with blooms to beautiful effect. Purple artichokes, almost black aubergines (eggplants), pink and white garlic bulbs, and bright red radishes can give depth, substance and a focal point to a variety of differnt arrangements.

Dried citrus fruit slices look wonderful, and will retain a slight tangy perfume.

17

COVERING A WIRE HANDLE WITH RIBBON

To make carrying a wired bouquet more comfortable the wired stems can be made into a handle.

1 To ensure that the handle is the correct length, trim it to about 1.5 cm (½ in) longer than the diagonal measurement across your palm. Cover the wire handle with florist's stem-wrap tape. Hold the bouquet in one hand and, with your thumb, trap a long length of 2.5 cm (1 in) wide ribbon against the binding point of the bouquet, leaving approximately a 10 cm (4 in) of ribbon above your thumb.

Take the long end of the ribbon down the handle, under its end and approximately half way up the other side. Hold it in place there with the little finger of your hand, making sure that your thumb remains firmly in place at the binding point.

2 Wind the ribbon back over itself, around and down the handle to its end. Next wind the ribbon back up the handle all the way to the binding point, covering the ribbon already in place and the tape on the handle.

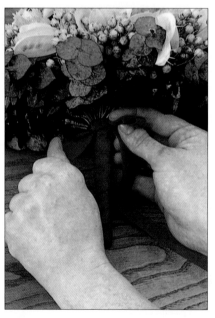

3 Take the winding end of the ribbon, and the excess 10 cm (4 in) at the other end, and tie in a knot at the binding point. Finish in a bow and trim the ribbon ends.

LINING A CONTAINER

If a container is to be used for arranging fresh flowers then clearly it must be watertight. However, if you are arranging your flowers in plastic foam then you can use a container which is not watertight provided you line it with polythene or cellophane (plastic wrap).

1 Cut a piece of cellophane (plastic wrap) slightly larger than the container and push it into the container making sure that it gets into all the corners and has no holes or tears. Cut the soaked plastic foam with a knife to fit the container and wedge it in. Trim the lining around the edge of the container and secure the plastic foam in place with florist's adhesive tape.

Be sure not to allow any water to get between the lining and the container and do not trim the lining too short as the water may spill over the top and down on to the sides.

SPIRALLING STEMS

A hand-tied spiralled bouquet is an excellent way of presenting flowers as a gift because they are already arranged and the recipient only has to cut the string and place the flowers in a suitable vase.

1 Place all the materials close to hand so that you can pick up individual stems easily. Hold a strong stem of foliage or flowers in one hand approximately two-thirds down from its top. Build the bouquet by adding one stem of your materials at a time, gradually turning the bunch in your hand as you do so to produce a spiral of stems. If you add your materials in a pre-planned repeating sequence, it will ensure an even distribution of different varieties throughout the bouquet. By occasionally varying the position you hold the stems as you add them it is possible to create a domed shape to the bunch.

2 When you have completed the bunch tie securely with twine, raffia or ribbon around the point where all the stems cross – the binding point.

3 Trim the stem ends so they are even, remembering that the stems below the binding point should comprise about one-third of the overall height of the finished bouquet.

STITCHING LEAVES

Stitching is a technique for wiring a leaf in such a way that it can be held in a "naturally" bent position.

1 Hold a leaf in one hand with its back facing you and very carefully stitch a thin wire horizontally through the central vein and back out again. You need to practise this a few times.

Bend the legs of the wire down along the stem forming a hairpin shape. Hold one leg of wire against the stem of the leaf and wrap the other leg of wire around both stem and wire several times. Then straighten the legs and tape with florist's tape (stem-wrap tape).

Below: Very fine reel wire can also be used to secure material to basket edgings.

CARE OF CUT FLOWERS

· · ·

CONDITIONING

Conditioning is the term for the process of preparing flowers and foliage for use in arranging.

The general rules are: remove all lower leaves to ensure there is no soft material below the water level where it will rot, form bacteria and shorten the life of the arrangement; cut the stem ends at an angle to provide as large a surface area as possible for the take-up of water; and, finally, stand all materials in cold water for a couple of hours to encourage the maximum intake of water before use.

For many varieties of flower and foliage this treatment is perfectly adequate; for some, however, there are a number of additional methods to increase their longevity.

BOILING WATER

The woody stems of lilac, guelder rose and rhododendron, the sap-filled stems of milkweed (euphorbia) and poppy, even roses and chrysan-themums, will benefit from the shock treatment of immersing their stem ends in boiling water.

Remove all lower foliage, together with approximately 6 cm (2½ in) of bark from the ends of woody stems. Cut the stem ends at an angle of 45 degrees and, in the case of woody stems, split up to approximately 6 cm (2½ in) from the bottom. Wrap any flowerheads in paper to protect them from the hot steam.

Carefully pour boiling water into a heatproof container to a depth of approximately 6 cm (2½ in) and plunge the bottoms of the stems into the hot water, leaving them for two to three minutes before removing and plunging them into deep cold water. The heat of the boiling water will have dispelled air from the stems to enable the efficient take-up of cold water. The boiling water will also have destroyed bacteria on the stem ends.

Wilted roses can also be revived by having their stems recut and given the boiling water treatment, and then left standing (with their heads wrapped up to their necks) in cold water for two hours.

The rose stripper (below) is invaluable when dealing with very thorny stems.

SEARING

Searing is a method of extending the lives of plants such as milkweed (euphorbia) and poppies which contain a milky sap, the release of which affects the water quality.

It involves passing the stem end through a flame until it is blackened, then placing it in tepid water. This forms a layer of charcoal to seal the stem end, preventing sap leakage but still allowing the take-up of water.

HOLLOW STEMS

Delphiniums, amaryllis (see *above*) and lupins have hollow stems and the best method of conditioning them is to turn them upside-down and literally fill them with water.

To keep the water in the stem, form a plug from cotton wool or tissue and carefully bung the open stem end. Tie a rubber band around the base of the stem to avoid splitting, then stand the stem in tepid water. The water trapped inside the stem will keep it firm and the cotton wool will help draw more water up into it.

FOLIAGE

Generally the rules for conditioning foliage are the same as for flowers. It is vital to strip the lower leaves and cut the stem base at an angle. Depending on the stem structure and size, other special techniques may well apply. It is also important to scrape the bark from the bottom 6 cm (2½ in) of the stem and split it to further encourage the take-up of water and thereby prolong the life of the foliage (see *below*).

WRAPPING TO STRAIGHTEN STEMS

Some flowers, such as gerbera, have soft, flexible weak stems and other flowers may simply have wilted. There is a technique for strengthening such material: take a group of flowers and wrap the top three-quarters of their stems together in paper to keep them erect, then stand them in deep cool water for about two hours (see *above*). The cells within the stems will fill with water and be able to stand on their own when the paper is removed.

ETHYLENE GAS

Ethylene is an odourless gas emitted by such things as rubbish (garbage), exhaust fumes, fungi and ripening fruit. It has the effect of accelerating the rate at which some flowers mature which in turn causes non-opening and dropping of buds and yellowing of leaves. Particularly susceptible are carnations, freesia, alstroemeria and roses. Be aware of this when using fruit in an arrangement (see *below*).

FLOWER AVAILABILITY CHART

· · ·

This list is an indication of current availability of the flowers from the Dutch market.
As development in production of individual varieties improve, this information may change.

✻✻✻ *good availability*   ✻✻ *some availability*   ✻ *limited availability*

FLOWER TYPE	JAN	FEB	MAR	APR	MAY	JUN	JUL	AUG	SEP	OCT	NOV	DEC	SPECIAL NOTES
Achillea			✻	✻	✻			✻✻✻	✻✻✻				*Some varieties only available in Spring*
Aconitum (monkshood)					✻			✻✻✻	✻✻✻				
Agapanthus	✻	✻						✻✻✻	✻✻✻	✻	✻	✻	*Some varieties moderately available in Winter*
Ageratum		✻			✻			✻✻✻	✻✻✻	✻✻✻	✻✻✻		
Alchemilla (mollis)							✻	✻					
Allium					✻			✻✻✻	✻✻✻				
Alstroemeria	✻✻✻	✻✻	✻✻	✻✻✻	✻✻✻	✻✻✻	✻✻✻	✻✻✻	✻✻✻	✻✻✻	✻✻✻	✻✻✻	*Some varieties not so available early Spring*
Amaranthus (red and green)	✻✻						✻✻	✻✻✻	✻✻✻	✻✻✻	✻✻✻	✻✻✻	
Amaryllis (Belladonna)	✻✻							✻✻	✻✻	✻✻✻	✻✻✻	✻✻✻	
Ammi majus (white dill)	✻✻✻	✻✻✻	✻✻✻	✻✻✻	✻✻✻	✻✻✻	✻✻✻	✻✻	✻✻	✻✻✻	✻✻✻	✻✻✻	
Anemones	✻✻✻	✻✻✻	✻✻✻	✻✻✻	✻✻✻	✻✻				✻✻✻	✻✻✻	✻✻✻	
Anethum graveolens (green dill)	✻✻				✻✻		✻✻	✻✻✻	✻✻✻	✻✻✻	✻✻✻		
Anigozanthus (kangaroo paw)	✻✻	✻✻	✻✻	✻✻	✻✻	✻✻	✻✻	✻✻	✻✻	✻✻	✻✻	✻✻	*Some varieties not available mid-Spring*
Anthuriums	✻✻✻	✻✻✻	✻✻✻	✻✻✻	✻✻✻	✻✻✻	✻✻✻	✻✻✻	✻✻✻	✻✻✻	✻✻✻	✻✻✻	*Most colours available throughout the year*
Antirrhinum majus	✻✻✻	✻✻✻	✻	✻✻✻	✻✻✻	✻✻✻	✻✻✻	✻✻✻	✻✻✻	✻✻✻	✻✻✻	✻✻✻	*Most colours not available in early Spring*
Asclepias	✻✻	✻✻✻	✻✻✻	✻✻✻	✻✻✻	✻✻✻	✻✻✻	✻✻✻	✻✻✻	✻✻✻	✻✻✻	✻✻✻	*A. incarnata only available early Autumn*
Asters	✻✻✻	✻✻✻					✻✻✻	✻✻✻	✻✻✻	✻✻✻	✻✻✻	✻✻✻	*Some varieties only available late Autumn*
Astilbe				✻	✻	✻		✻✻✻	✻✻✻	✻✻✻	✻✻✻	✻✻✻	*A. 'Whasingthon' only available late Spring*
Astrantia									✻	✻	✻		
Atriplex	✻✻	✻✻✻	✻✻✻	✻✻✻	✻✻✻	✻✻			✻✻	✻✻	✻✻	✻✻	
Bouvardia	✻✻✻	✻✻✻	✻✻✻	✻✻✻	✻✻✻	✻✻✻	✻✻✻	✻✻✻	✻✻✻	✻✻✻	✻✻✻	✻✻✻	*B. longiflorum not available in Spring*
Bupleurum griffithii	✻✻✻	✻✻✻	✻	✻✻✻	✻✻✻	✻✻✻	✻✻✻	✻✻✻	✻✻✻	✻✻✻	✻✻✻	✻✻✻	
Callistephus (China aster)			✻	✻	✻			✻✻✻	✻✻✻	✻✻✻	✻✻✻	✻✻✻	
Campanula					✻✻✻	✻✻✻	✻✻✻						
Carthamus	✻✻	✻✻	✻✻	✻✻			✻✻	✻✻✻	✻✻✻	✻✻✻	✻✻✻	✻✻✻	
Celosia	✻✻	✻✻						✻✻✻	✻✻✻	✻✻✻	✻✻✻	✻✻✻	
Centaurea cyanus (cornflower)								✻✻✻	✻✻✻	✻✻✻	✻✻✻		
Centaurea macrocephala								✻	✻				
Chamelaucium (waxflower)		✻✻	✻✻	✻✻	✻✻								
Chelone obliqua					✻✻	✻✻			✻✻✻	✻✻✻	✻✻✻		
Chrysanthemum santini	✻✻✻	✻✻✻	✻✻✻	✻✻✻	✻✻✻	✻✻✻	✻✻✻	✻✻✻	✻✻✻	✻✻✻	✻✻✻	✻✻✻	
Chrysanthemum (Indicum gr.)	✻✻✻	✻✻✻	✻✻✻	✻✻✻	✻✻✻	✻✻✻	✻✻✻	✻✻✻	✻✻✻	✻✻✻	✻✻✻	✻✻✻	
Cirsium		✻✻	✻✻			✻✻	✻✻✻	✻✻✻	✻✻✻	✻✻✻	✻✻✻	✻✻	
Convallaria majalis (lily-of-the-valley)	✻✻	✻✻	✻✻	✻✻	✻✻	✻✻	✻✻	✻✻	✻✻	✻✻	✻✻	✻✻	
Crocosmia (Montbretia)							✻✻✻	✻✻✻	✻✻✻				
Cyclamen	✻✻✻	✻✻✻	✻✻✻	✻✻✻	✻✻✻	✻✻✻						✻✻✻	
Cymbidium orchids	✻✻✻	✻✻✻	✻✻✻	✻✻✻	✻✻✻	✻✻✻		✻✻✻		✻✻✻	✻✻✻	✻✻✻	
Dahlias								✻✻✻	✻✻✻	✻✻✻	✻✻✻	✻✻✻	
Delphinium ajacis (larkspur)	✻✻✻	✻✻✻	✻✻✻	✻✻✻	✻✻✻	✻✻✻	✻✻✻	✻✻✻	✻✻✻	✻✻✻	✻✻✻	✻✻✻	
Delphinium	✻✻	✻✻	✻✻	✻✻	✻✻✻	✻✻✻	✻✻✻	✻✻✻	✻✻✻	✻✻✻	✻✻✻	✻✻✻	
Dendrobium orchids	✻✻✻	✻✻✻	✻✻✻	✻✻✻	✻✻✻	✻✻✻	✻✻✻	✻✻✻	✻✻✻	✻✻✻	✻✻✻	✻✻✻	
Dianthus barbatus (sweet william)	✻	✻	✻✻	✻✻✻	✻✻✻	✻✻✻	✻✻✻	✻	✻	✻	✻		
Dianthus (standard carnation)	✻✻✻	✻✻✻	✻✻✻	✻✻✻	✻✻✻	✻✻✻	✻✻✻	✻✻✻	✻✻✻	✻✻✻	✻✻✻	✻✻✻	
Dianthus (spray carnation)	✻✻✻	✻✻✻	✻✻✻	✻✻✻	✻✻✻	✻✻✻	✻✻✻	✻✻✻	✻✻✻	✻✻✻	✻✻✻	✻✻✻	
Echinops								✻✻✻	✻✻✻	✻✻✻	✻✻✻		
Eremurus stenophyllus (fox tail lily)						✻✻✻	✻✻✻	✻✻✻	✻✻✻	✻	✻		
Eryngium	✻✻✻	✻✻✻						✻✻✻	✻✻✻	✻✻✻	✻✻✻	✻✻✻	
Eupatorium								✻✻✻	✻✻✻	✻✻✻			
Euphorbia fulgens	✻✻✻	✻✻✻	✻✻✻							✻✻✻	✻✻✻	✻✻✻	
Eustoma russellianum	✻✻✻	✻✻✻					✻✻✻	✻✻✻	✻✻✻	✻✻✻	✻✻✻	✻✻✻	
Forsythia intermedia			✻✻✻	✻✻✻	✻✻✻	✻✻✻							
Freesia	✻✻✻	✻✻✻	✻✻✻	✻✻✻	✻✻✻	✻✻✻	✻✻✻	✻✻✻	✻✻✻	✻✻✻	✻✻✻	✻✻✻	
Gerbera	✻✻✻	✻✻✻	✻✻✻	✻✻✻	✻✻✻	✻✻✻	✻✻✻	✻✻✻	✻✻✻	✻✻✻	✻✻✻	✻✻✻	
Gladioli								✻✻✻	✻✻✻	✻✻✻	✻✻✻	✻✻✻	

Flower Type	Jan	Feb	Mar	Apr	May	Jun	Jul	Aug	Sep	Oct	Nov	Dec	Special Notes
Gloriosa rothschildiana (glory lily)	✽✽✽	✽✽✽	✽✽	✽✽✽	✽✽✽	✽✽✽	✽✽✽	✽✽✽	✽✽✽	✽✽✽	✽✽✽	✽✽✽	
Godetia	✽✽✽			✽✽✽	✽✽✽	✽✽✽	✽✽✽	✽✽✽	✽✽✽	✽✽✽	✽✽✽	✽✽✽	
Gomphrena	✽✽	✽✽						✽✽	✽✽✽	✽✽✽	✽✽✽	✽✽✽	
Gypsophila	✽✽✽	✽✽✽	✽✽✽	✽✽✽	✽✽✽	✽✽✽	✽✽✽	✽✽✽	✽✽✽	✽✽✽	✽✽✽	✽✽✽	
Helenium								✽✽✽	✽✽✽	✽✽✽	✽✽✽	✽✽✽	
Helianthus (sunflower)						✽✽✽	✽✽✽	✽✽✽	✽✽✽	✽✽✽	✽✽✽	✽✽	
Heliconia	✽✽✽	✽✽✽	✽✽✽	✽✽✽	✽✽✽	✽✽✽	✽✽	✽✽	✽✽	✽✽	✽✽✽	✽✽✽	
Hippeastrum	✽✽✽	✽✽✽	✽✽✽	✽✽✽	✽✽✽	✽✽✽	✽✽✽			✽✽✽	✽✽✽	✽✽✽	
Hyacinths		✽✽	✽✽✽	✽✽✽	✽✽✽	✽✽✽	✽✽						
Hydrangea	✽✽	✽✽	✽✽	✽✽	✽✽	✽✽	✽✽✽	✽✽✽	✽✽	✽✽	✽✽	✽✽	
Hypericum	✽✽	✽✽						✽✽	✽✽	✽✽✽	✽✽✽	✽✽✽	
Iris	✽✽✽	✽✽✽	✽✽✽	✽✽✽	✽✽✽	✽✽✽	✽✽✽	✽✽✽	✽✽✽	✽✽✽	✽✽✽	✽✽✽	
Ixia					✽	✽							
Kniphofia (red hot pokers)						✽✽	✽✽	✽✽	✽	✽	✽	✽✽	
Lathyrus (sweet peas)			✽	✽	✽✽	✽✽	✽✽✽	✽✽✽					
Leucanthemum	✽✽✽	✽✽✽	✽✽✽	✽✽✽	✽✽✽	✽✽✽	✽✽✽	✽✽✽	✽✽✽	✽✽✽	✽✽✽	✽✽✽	
Liatris	✽✽✽	✽✽✽	✽✽✽	✽✽✽	✽✽✽	✽✽✽	✽✽✽	✽✽✽	✽✽✽	✽✽✽	✽✽✽	✽✽✽	
Lilium	✽✽✽	✽✽✽	✽✽✽	✽✽✽	✽✽✽	✽✽✽	✽✽✽	✽✽✽	✽✽✽	✽✽✽	✽✽✽	✽✽✽	
Limonium (stratice)	✽✽✽	✽✽✽	✽✽✽	✽✽✽	✽✽✽	✽✽✽	✽✽✽	✽✽✽	✽✽✽	✽✽✽	✽✽✽	✽✽✽	
Lysimachia clethroides		✽✽✽	✽✽✽	✽✽✽	✽✽✽	✽✽✽	✽✽✽	✽✽✽	✽✽✽	✽✽✽	✽✽✽	✽✽✽	
Lysimachia vulgaris	✽✽	✽✽							✽✽✽	✽✽✽	✽✽	✽✽	
Matthiola incana (stocks)	✽	✽	✽	✽	✽✽✽	✽✽✽	✽✽✽	✽✽✽	✽✽	✽✽	✽✽	✽	A white variety is available all year
Mentha (flowering mint)									✽✽✽	✽✽✽	✽✽✽		
Molucella laevis (bells of Ireland)	✽✽✽	✽✽✽	✽✽✽	✽✽✽	✽✽✽	✽✽✽	✽✽✽	✽✽✽	✽✽✽	✽✽✽	✽✽✽	✽✽✽	
Muscari (grape hyacinth)	✽✽	✽✽✽	✽✽✽	✽✽✽	✽✽✽	✽✽✽	✽✽					✽✽	
Narcissi		✽✽✽	✽✽✽	✽✽✽	✽✽✽	✽✽✽							
Nerine	✽✽✽	✽✽✽	✽✽✽	✽✽✽	✽✽✽	✽✽✽	✽✽✽	✽✽✽	✽✽✽	✽✽✽	✽✽✽	✽✽✽	
Oenothera								✽✽✽					
Oncidium (golden showers orchid)	✽✽✽	✽✽✽	✽✽✽	✽✽✽	✽✽✽	✽✽✽	✽✽✽	✽✽✽	✽✽✽	✽✽✽	✽✽✽	✽✽✽	
Origanum								✽✽✽	✽✽✽	✽✽✽	✽✽✽	✽✽✽	
Ornithogalum arabicum (Moroccan chincherinchee)	✽✽	✽✽	✽✽✽	✽✽✽	✽✽✽	✽✽✽	✽✽	✽✽	✽✽	✽✽	✽✽	✽✽✽	
Ornithagalum thyrsoides (chincherinchee)	✽✽✽	✽✽✽	✽✽✽	✽✽✽	✽✽✽	✽✽✽		✽✽✽	✽✽✽			✽✽✽	
Peonies						✽✽✽	✽✽✽	✽✽✽					
Papaver (poppy seed heads)								✽✽✽	✽✽✽	✽✽✽	✽✽✽	✽✽✽	
Paphiopedilum (orchid)	✽✽✽	✽✽✽	✽✽✽	✽✽		✽✽	✽✽	✽✽	✽✽	✽✽	✽✽		
Phalaenopsis (orchid)	✽✽✽	✽✽✽	✽✽✽	✽✽✽	✽✽✽	✽✽✽	✽✽✽	✽✽✽	✽✽✽	✽✽✽	✽✽✽	✽✽✽	
Phlox	✽✽✽	✽✽✽	✽✽✽	✽✽✽	✽✽✽	✽✽✽	✽✽✽	✽✽✽	✽✽✽	✽✽✽	✽✽✽	✽✽✽	
Physostegia (obedient plant)								✽	✽	✽	✽		
Protea	✽✽✽	✽✽✽	✽✽✽			✽✽						✽✽✽	
Prunus	✽✽	✽✽✽	✽✽✽	✽✽✽	✽✽✽	✽✽							
Ranunculus		✽✽	✽✽	✽✽✽	✽✽✽	✽✽✽	✽✽✽						
Roses	✽✽✽	✽✽✽	✽✽✽	✽✽✽	✽✽✽	✽✽✽	✽✽✽	✽✽✽	✽✽✽	✽✽✽	✽✽✽	✽✽✽	
Saponaria								✽✽✽	✽✽✽	✽✽✽	✽✽✽		
Scabious								✽✽✽	✽✽✽	✽✽✽	✽✽✽		
Scilla (bluebells)			✽✽✽	✽✽✽	✽✽✽								
Sedum spectabile								✽✽✽	✽✽✽	✽✽✽	✽✽✽		
Solidago	✽✽✽	✽✽✽	✽✽✽	✽✽✽	✽✽✽	✽✽✽	✽✽✽	✽✽✽	✽✽✽	✽✽✽	✽✽✽	✽✽✽	
Strelitzia	✽✽✽	✽✽✽	✽✽✽	✽✽✽	✽✽✽	✽✽✽	✽✽✽	✽✽✽	✽✽✽	✽✽✽	✽✽✽	✽✽✽	
Symphoricarpos (snowberry)									✽✽✽	✽✽✽	✽✽✽	✽✽✽	
Syringa (lilac)	✽✽✽	✽✽✽	✽✽✽	✽✽✽	✽✽✽	✽✽						✽✽✽	
Tanacetum (feverfew)	✽✽✽	✽✽✽	✽✽✽	✽✽✽	✽✽✽	✽✽✽	✽✽✽	✽✽✽	✽✽✽	✽✽✽	✽✽✽	✽✽✽	
Trachelium	✽✽✽	✽✽✽	✽✽✽	✽✽✽	✽✽✽	✽✽✽	✽✽✽	✽✽✽	✽✽✽	✽✽✽	✽✽✽	✽✽✽	White Trachelium not available early Spring
Triteleia (Brodiaea)						✽✽✽	✽✽✽	✽✽✽	✽✽✽	✽✽✽			
Tulips	✽✽	✽✽	✽✽✽	✽✽✽	✽✽✽	✽✽✽	✽✽					✽✽	
Veronica	✽✽✽	✽✽✽	✽✽✽	✽✽✽	✽✽✽	✽✽✽	✽✽✽	✽✽✽	✽✽✽	✽✽✽	✽✽✽	✽✽✽	
Viburnum opulus (guelder rose)	✽✽	✽✽	✽✽✽	✽✽✽	✽✽✽	✽✽✽	✽✽	✽✽					
Zantedeschia aethiopica (arum lily)	✽✽	✽✽	✽✽✽	✽✽✽	✽✽✽	✽✽✽	✽✽✽	✽✽✽	✽✽✽	✽✽✽	✽✽✽	✽✽	
Zantedeschia (calla lily)	✽✽✽	✽✽✽	✽✽✽	✽✽✽	✽✽✽	✽✽✽	✽✽✽	✽✽✽	✽✽✽	✽✽✽			
Zinnia								✽✽✽	✽✽✽	✽✽			

TULIP ARRANGEMENT

· · ·

MATERIALS

· · ·

50 'Angelique' tulips

· · ·

scissors

· · ·

watertight container, e.g. small bucket

· · ·

basket

The arrangement is technically relatively unstructured but, by repetition of the regular form of the tulip heads, the overall visual effect is that of a formal dome of flowers to be viewed in the round.

Sometimes the simple beauty of an arrangement which relies entirely on one type of flower in its own foliage can be breathtaking. This display of Angelique tulips in glorious profusion contains nothing to compete with their soft pastel pink colour and would make a dramatic room centrepiece.

1 Strip the lower leaves from the tulips to prevent them from rotting in the water. Fill the bucket with water and place in the basket.

2 Cut each tulip stem to the correct size and place the stems in the water. Arrange them to start building the display from its lowest circumference upwards.

3 Continue arranging the tulips towards the centre of the display until a full and even domed shape is achieved. The display should be able to be viewed from all sides.

BLUE AND WHITE TUSSIE MUSSIES

· · ·

Small, hand-tied spiralled posies make perfect gifts and, in the right vase, ideal centre decorations for small tables. Both of these displays have delicate flowers massed together. One features Japanese anemones, visually strengthened by blackberries on stems; the other delphiniums supported by rosehip stems.

MATERIALS
· · ·
TUSSIE 1 (on left)
· · ·
blackberries on stems
· · ·
white Japanese anemones
· · ·
1 stem draceana
· · ·
twine
· · ·
ribbon
· · ·
scissors
· · ·
TUSSIE 2 (on right)
· · ·
4-5 stems 'Blue Butterfly' delphinium
· · ·
3 stems rosehips
· · ·
5 small Virginia creeper leaves
· · ·
twine
· · ·
ribbon
· · ·
scissors

Whilst the flowers need to be tightly massed for the best effect, they have relatively large but fragile blooms, so take care not to crush their petals, and tie off firmly but gently.

1 Start with a central flower and add stems of foliage and flowers, turning the posy in your hand to build the design into a spiral.

2 Once all the ingredients have been used, and the bunch is completed, tie firmly at the binding point with twine. Repeat steps one and two for the second tussie mussie.

3 Trim the ends of the flower stems with scissors to achieve a neat edge. Finish both tussie mussies with a ribbon bow.

HEAVILY SCENTED ARRANGEMENT

· · ·

MATERIALS

· · ·

1 block plastic foam

· · ·

cellophane (plastic wrap)

· · ·

wooden trug

· · ·

scissors

· · ·

20 stems golden privet

· · ·

10 stems tuberose

· · ·

10 stems cream stocks

· · ·

20 stems freesias

· · ·

20 stems mimosa

Mimosa has a substantial main stem with slender offshoots. For greater flexibility, remove the offshoots and discard the heavier main stem.

The flowers used in this display are chosen for their distinctive and delicious scents, which combine to produce a heady perfume guaranteed to silence those who claim that commercially-grown blooms do not have the fragrance of their garden equivalents. It is an ideal arrangement for a hallway or living room where the scent will be most attractive.

The outline of the display is established in golden privet reinforced with waxy tuberose and soft-textured stocks. These provide a cream and yellow backdrop for the focal flowers, pale yellow, double-petalled freesias. The whole arrangement is visually co-ordinated by the introduction of the soft green, feathery foliage and powdery yellow flowers of mimosa.

1 Firmly wedge a water-soaked block of plastic foam into a cellophane-lined (plastic wrap-lined) trug. Trim the excess cellophane from the edge of the trug. (If the finished arrangement is likely to be moved secure the plastic foam in the trug with florist's adhesive tape.)

2 First ensuring the leaves are stripped from the stem bottoms, insert the golden privet into the foam to build the outline of the arrangement. Because they make small neat holes, the slender stems of golden privet are ideal for arranging in plastic foam.

3 Reinforce the outline of the display with the tuberose and the stocks, arranging them in opposite diagonals.

4 Distribute the freesias throughout the display, using stems with buds to the outside and more open blooms to the centre. Break off the mimosa's offshoots so that a mixture of stem sizes can be arranged through the display which will visually pull everything together.

HYACINTH BULB VASES

· · ·

Bulbs can be grown in water as well as in soil. By employing this technique and with some long-term planning, the commonplace hyacinth has been given a new interest in this display.

MATERIALS

· · ·

3 bulb vases

· · ·

2 jam jars

· · ·

4 thin sturdy twigs

· · ·

raffia

· · ·

scissors

· · ·

5 hyacinth bulbs

There are vases expressly made for water-growing bulbs and some of the old-fashioned types are particularly attractive – so search your local junk and antique shops. At the same time, a simple jam jar, with a twig frame to support the bulb, will do the job just as well. This particular arrangement is a grouping of both types of container, which are as important to the overall success of the display as the flowers themselves.

1 If you are using bulb vases, simply fill each one with water and place the bulbs on the top with their bases sitting in the water. Top up the water occasionally, taking care not to disturb the roots. Then just wait until the hyacinth bulbs root, grow and flower!

2 The use of a jam jar requires making a square frame to sit on top of the jar. Use thin but sturdy twigs firmly tied together with raffia to form the frame. Trim the stem ends and the raffia when you have established that the frame fits the jar neatly, then position the bulb on the frame with its base in the water.

SPRING NAPKIN DECORATION

· · ·

The sophisticated gold and white colour combination used in these elegant and delicate napkin decorations would be perfect for a formal dinner or an important occasion such as a wedding.

In addition to its exquisite scent, the tiny bells of lily-of-the-valley visually harmonize with the pure white of the cyclamen.

MATERIALS

· · ·

napkins

· · ·

*small-leaved ivy
trails (sprigs)*

· · ·

scissors

· · ·

1 pot lily-of-the-valley

· · ·

*1 pot tiny cyclamen (dwarf
Cyclamen persicum)*

· · ·

gold cord

The slender stems of both flowers enable each decoration to be made into a tied sheaf. The splayed stems echo the shape made by the flowers.

1 Fold the napkin into a rectangle, then roll into a cylindrical shape. Wrap an ivy trail (sprig) around the middle of the napkin. Tie the stem firmly in a knot.

2 Take 4–5 stems of lily-of-the-valley, 3 flowers of cyclamen on their stems and 3 cyclamen leaves. Using both flowers, create a small flat-backed sheaf in your hand by spiralling the stems. Place one leaf at the back of the lily-of-the-valley for support and use the other two around the cyclamen flowers to emphasize the focal point. Tie at the binding point with gold cord. Lay the flat back of the sheaf on top of the napkin and ivy, wrap the excess gold cord around the napkin, gently tying into a bow on top of the stems.

FRESH HERBAL WREATH

· · ·

MATERIALS

· · ·

30 cm (12 in) plastic foam wreath frame

· · ·

scissors

· · ·

2 branches bay leaves

· · ·

2 bunches rosemary

· · ·

.71 wires

· · ·

6 large bulbs (heads) garlic

· · ·

6 or 7 beetroot (beets)

· · ·

40 stems flowering marjoram

· · ·

40 stems flowering mint

As well as being decorative, a herb wreath can also be useful. The herbs can be taken from it and used in the kitchen without causing too much damage to the overall design.

In many parts of Europe it is believed that a herb wreath hung in a kitchen, or by the entrance of a house, is a sign of welcome, wealth and good luck. This wreath will stay fresh for two or three weeks because the stems of the herbs are in water, but even if it dries out it will continue to look good for some time.

1 Soak the wreath frame thoroughly in cold water. Create the background by making a foliage outline using evenly distributed bay leaves and sprigs of rosemary. To ensure an even covering, position the leaves inside, on top and on the outside of the wreath frame.

2 Wire the garlic bulbs (heads) and beetroot (beets) by pushing two wires through their base so that they cross, then pull the projecting wires down and cut to the correct length for the depth of the foam. Decide where on the wreath they are to be positioned and push the wires firmly into the foam.

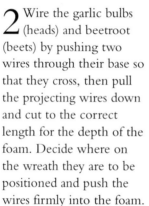

3 Infill the spaces in the wreath, concentrating the marjoram around the beetroot and the mint around the garlic.

SPRING BLOSSOM URN

· · ·

MATERIALS

· · ·

urn

· · ·

cellophane (plastic wrap)

· · ·

1 block plastic foam

· · ·

scissors

· · ·

.71 wires

· · ·

reindeer moss

· · ·

15 stems pussy willow

· · ·

10 stems white lilac

· · ·

15 stems pink cherry blossom

The bright, fresh arrangement joyously leaping out of a cold, hard, metal urn, symbolizes the winter soil erupting with spring growth.

The explosion of plant life in the spring is visually depicted in this arrangement of early flowers and foliage.

Heavily flowered heads of white lilac are the focal blossoms of the display set against the dark brown stems of pussy willow and cherry. The starkness of these stems is softened by the emerging pink blossom of the cherry and the furry silver pussy willow buds, both of which harmonize with the lilac.

1 Line the urn with cellophane (plastic wrap) and wedge in the water-soaked block of plastic foam. Trim away the excess cellophane.

2 Make hairpins from .71 wires and pin reindeer moss into the plastic foam around the rim of the urn. Make sure that the foam is entirely covered on all sides.

3 Arrange the pussy willow in the urn to establish the height and width of a symmetrical outline. Press the pussy willow stems firmly into the plastic foam to secure the arrangement.

4 Distribute the lilac throughout the pussy willow. Look carefully at the way lilac flowers hang from their stems and try to exploit their natural attitude in the arrangement. You will find there is no need to position the stems at extreme angles.

5 Position the pink cherry blossom throughout the display to reinforce the overall shape and provide a link between the slender stems of pussy willow and the large heads of the flowering lilac.

HYACINTH BULB BOWL
. . .

MATERIALS
. . .
8 sprouting hyacinth bulbs
. . .
24 autumn leaves
. . .
raffia
. . .
scissors
. . .
glass bowl

This novel approach to the display of developing hyacinth bulbs takes them out of their pots and into organic containers which become feature elements in the design. This attractive display will last for many weeks.

The bulbs' roots, along with their soil, are simply wrapped in leaves and then grouped together sitting in water in a glass bowl. The bulbs take up the water and happily grow from these attractive green spikes through to full flowers.

1 Carefully remove the hyacinth bulbs from their pots, keeping the soil tightly packed around the roots. Wrap a leaf underneath the root ball and soil of each bulb, with two more leaves around the sides. Leave the majority of each bulb exposed as it would be in a pot.

2 Secure the leaves in position by tying around with raffia. Group the wrapped hyacinths in the glass bowl and fill to approximately 5 cm (2 in) deep with water. Remember to top up regularly. The bulbs will continue to grow and eventually bloom.

NAPKIN TIE

· · ·

This beautiful alternative to a napkin ring is easy to make and very effective in enhancing the look of your dinner table. Its appearance can be changed to suit many different occasions.

1 Find a suitable length of rosemary, long and flexible enough to wrap around the rolled napkin once or twice. Tie the stem securely.

2 Arrange the lemon geranium leaves and mint flowerheads by gently pushing the stems through the knot of the binding rosemary stem.

MATERIALS

· · ·

napkin

· · ·

scissors

· · ·

long, thin, flexible stem rosemary

· · ·

3 lemon geranium leaves

· · ·

2 or 3 heads flowering mint

The method is simply to use any reasonably sturdy trailing foliage to bind the napkin and then create a focal point by the addition of leaves, berries or flowerheads of your choice. If a firm fixing is required, wire the leaves and flowerheads before attaching to binding material.

TULIP POMANDER

· · ·

MATERIALS

· · ·

1 plastic foam ball

· · ·

ribbon

· · ·

scissors

· · ·

*20 heads 'Appleblossom'
double tulips*

· · ·

1 bunch myrtle

· · ·

.71 wires

· · ·

*a good handful
reindeer moss*

*The pomander illustrated does
not boast exotic aromas but it
does have a pleasing variety of
surface textures, ranging from
the spiky inner petals of double
tulips through the beady black
berries of myrtle to the softness
of grey moss, all set against
bands of smooth satin ribbon.*

In Elizabethan times pomanders were filled with herbs or scented flowers and carried to perfume the air. Today the pomander is more likely to be a bridesmaid's accessory, a charming alternative to the conventional posy.

1 Soak the foam ball in water. Tie the ribbon around the ball, starting at the top and crossing at the bottom, and then tying at the top to divide the ball into four equal segments. Make sure there is enough excess ribbon to tie into a bow.

2 Cut the tulips to a stem length of about 2.5 cm (1 in) and push into the foam in vertical lines at the centre of each segment. Hold the tulip heads gently while positioning them on the foam ball to avoid the heads breaking off.

3 Cut sprigs of myrtle on short stems and push into the foam to form lines on either side of each line of tulips. The myrtle should appear quite compact.

4 Form hairpins from the .71 wires and use them to pin the reindeer moss to cover all remaining exposed areas of the foam ball.

36

AMARYLLIS LINE ARRANGEMENT

• • •

MATERIALS

• • •

pinholder

• • •

shallow bowl

• • •

scissors

• • •

5 stems amaryllis

• • •

6 Phormium cookiannum
variagatum *leaves*

• • •

glass marbles

The amaryllis has an extraordinary-looking stem which, though hollow, is large and fleshy and carries heavy blooms. Plastic foam will not support a flower of this size and weight unless used in large amounts, reinforced with wire mesh with the amaryllis stem firmly staked.

The pinholder will give the amaryllis the secure support it requires because the fleshy stems can be pushed firmly on to the pins. Furthermore, the weight of the pinholder is sufficient to counterbalance the weight of the blooms.

A line arrangement is just that: a display of flowers in a staggered vertical line. The large blooms of the amaryllis are particularly suitable and here they are reinforced by the spiky leaves of *Phormium cookiannum variagatum*.

1 Place the pinholder in the centre of the bowl and completely cover it with water. Arrange the amaryllis in a staggered vertical line by pushing the stems on to the pins. Position the more closed blooms on longer stems towards the rear, and more open blooms with shorter stems towards the front of the arrangement. (Any spare flowerheads on short stems should be recessed into the base of the display by securing them on pins.)

2 Arrange the leaves, with the largest at the back and shortest to the front, in a diagonal through the staggered vertical line of amaryllis.

3 To complete the display, place it in its final position and conceal the top of the pinholder by scattering glass marbles on top of it.

NOSEGAYS
· · ·

Popular in Elizabethan times for warding off unpleasant smells, today nosegays, or tussie mussies, still make charming decorations and lovely gifts. The instructions are for the posy on the right of the main picture.

MATERIALS
· · ·
1 chive flower
· · ·
flowering mint
· · ·
rosemary
· · ·
fennel
· · ·
lemon geranium leaves
· · ·
twine
· · ·
scissors
· · ·
raffia

1 Cut all the plant stems to a length suitable for the size of posy you are making and clean them of leaves and thorns. Starting by holding the central flowers in your hand, add stems of the chosen herb, turning the emerging bunch as you work. Make sure you complete a circle with one herb before you start another. Finally use a circle of lemon geranium leaves to edge the bunch.

2 When everything is in position, tie with twine and trim stem ends neatly. Finish each nosegay with raffia tied in a bow.

These tiny herbal posies are made up of tight concentric circles of herbs around a central flower, which will exude a marvellous mix of scents and can be used for culinary as well as decorative purposes. Alternatively they can be left to dry, to provide lasting pleasure.

FRUIT AND FLOWER SWAG

· · ·

MATERIALS

· · ·

.71 wires

· · ·

4 limes

· · ·

9 lemons

· · ·

4 bunches black grapes

· · ·

*4 bunches sneezeweed
(Helenium)*

· · ·

1 bundle tree ivy

· · ·

scissors

· · ·

*straw plait (braid), about
60 cm (24 in) long*

· · ·

raffia

· · ·

1 bunch ivy trails (sprigs)

*The component parts have to
be wired, but otherwise the
swag is simple to construct. Do
remember that although lemons
and limes will survive in this
situation, grapes and cut
flowers will need regular mist
spraying with water.*

The colour and content of this decorative swag will brighten any room. Its visual freshness makes it especially suitable for a kitchen but, if it was made on a longer base, the decoration could be a mantelpiece garland or even extended to adorn the balustrade of a staircase.

1 First, all the fruit has to be wired. Pass a wire through from side to side just above the base of the limes. Leave equal lengths of wire projecting from either side, bend these down and twist together under the base. If the lemons are heavier than the limes, pass a second wire through at right angles to the first, providing four equal ends to be twisted together under their bases.

2 Group the grapes in small clusters and double leg mount with .71 wires. Then form 12 small bunches of sneezeweed mixed with tree ivy and double leg mount these on .71 wires.

3 Starting at its bottom end, bind three wired lemons to the plait (braid) with raffia. Then in turn bind a bunch of flowers and foliage, a lime, grapes and a second bunch of flowers and foliage.

4 Repeat binding materials to the plait in the above sequence until almost at the top. Secure by wrapping the remaining raffia tightly around the plait

5 Make a bow from raffia and tie to the top of the swag. Trim off any stray wire ends. Entwine the ivy trails (sprigs) around the top of the swag and bow.

PINK PHLOX ARRANGEMENT
IN A PITCHER

• • •

MATERIALS

• • •

scissors

• • •

15 stems pink phlox
'Bright Eyes'

• • •

pitcher

• • •

5 trails (sprigs) of Virginia
creeper in autumn tints

A simple-to-arrange pitcher of
flowers and foliage becomes an
explosion of colour and scent.

The colour collision between a mass of pink phlox flowerheads and the vibrant autumn reds of Virginia creeper gives this arrangement its visual impact and is a simple, yet effective arrangement to create.

1 Cut the stems of phlox to a length proportionate to the container. Arrange the phlox evenly with taller stems towards the back of the pitcher.

2 Place the cut ends of Virginia creeper trails (sprigs) in the pitcher of water and weave them through the heads of phlox, spreading them out evenly.

CANDLE RING

• • •

This pretty little candle ring is created on a very small diameter plastic foam ring. Filled with a heady combination of fennel, rosemary, lemon geranium, hyssop and violas, it would be perfect for an intimate dinner table.

MATERIALS

• • •

15 cm (6 in) diameter plastic foam ring

• • •

candlestick

• • •

scissors

• • •

small quantities of rosemary, lemon geranium leaves, fennel, hyssop and violas

The floral ring is simply placed over the candlestick to create this simple but effective decoration. Never leave a burning candle unattended and do not allow it to burn down to within less than 5 cm (2 in) of the foliage.

1 Soak the plastic foam ring in cold water and place it over the candlestick. Start the arrangement by making a basic outline in the plastic foam with stems of rosemary and geranium leaves, positioning them evenly around the ring. Try to arrange the leaves at different angles to produce a fuller effect.

2 Infill the gaps evenly with the fennel and hyssop, finally add a few violas for colour.

43

EXOTIC FLOWER ARRANGEMENT

· · ·

MATERIALS
· · ·
large fish bowl
· · ·
scissors
· · ·
5 stems contorted willow
· · ·
5 ginger flowers
· · ·
10 lotus seed heads
· · ·
7 celosia heads
· · ·
2 pink pineapples
· · ·
10 stems glory lily
· · ·
5 fishtail palms
· · ·
5 anthuriums
· · ·
7 Phormium tenax 'Bronze baby'
· · ·
6 small bunches of bear grass (Xerophyllum tenax)
· · ·
6 passion flower trails (sprays)

Most of the flowers and foliage in this display can subsequently be dried.

The apparent delicacy of some of the flowers in this spectacular arrangement belies their robust nature. Commercially-produced, exotic cut flowers not only look fabulous but also have a long life span.

1 Three-quarter fill the fish bowl with cold water. Cut the contorted willow stems to about three times the height of the vase and arrange to form the framework of the display.

2 Add the ginger flowers and lotus seedheads so that the tallest is slightly shorter than the contorted willow and placed at the back, with stems of decreasing height positioned to the front and sides.

3 Distribute the celosia through the display in the same way as the ginger flowers and lotus heads. Recess the two pink pineapples in the centre of the arrangement, leaving one taller than the other.

4 Position the glory lilies through the arrangement concentrating on the front and sides where they will naturally overhang the container. Arrange the anthuriums, which are the focal flowers, with tallest to the back becoming shorter to the front.

5 Untypically the foliage is added last. Distribute the individual exotic leaves and bunches of bear grass throughout the arrangement. Push the cut ends of the passion flower trails (sprays) into the back of the fish bowl and drape them down and around over the front.

ORCHID POSY

· · ·

MATERIALS

· · ·

6 stems orange/brown spotted spray orchid

· · ·

6 stems pink spotted spray orchid

· · ·

bear grass

· · ·

scissors

· · ·

twine

This tied posy is spiralled in the hand and contains just two varieties of orchid with fronds of bear grass. The strong stems of orchids are ideal for the spiralling technique and allow the finished posy to stand on its own and still keep its shape. The elegance of the bear grass helps the overall design by softening the solid outlines of the fleshy flowerheads.

The orchid grows in a multiplicity of shapes and colours, from delicate spray forms to large fleshy varieties. All orchids look exotic and can easily upstage other more subtle blooms in an arrangement. It follows that the orchid is most effective when used on its own in a single variety, or perhaps with other compatible varieties and some carefully chosen foliage.

1 Starting with a central orchid stem held in your hand, add flower stems and foliage to form a spiral. Separate the bear grass into slim bunches for easy handling.

2 Keep turning the posy in your hand as you add the stems, not forgetting to include the bunches of bear grass, until the arrangement is complete. Trim the stems.

3 Using the twine, tie the finished bunch at the binding point – i.e. where all the stems cross. Finish the posy by tying bear grass around the binding point to conceal the twine.

EXOTIC BUD VASE

· · ·

A selection of small colourful vases forms the basis of this attractive display of short-stemmed exotic flowers. Only one type of flower is used for each jar. Some have a single stem with a particular sculptural quality; others have flowers massed for colour and texture impact. It is a simple, effective display which relies as much on the choice of containers as the flowers used.

MATERIALS

· · ·

1 anthurium

· · ·

1 pink pineapple

· · ·

contorted willow stems

· · ·

3 exotic leaves

· · ·

3 celosia heads

· · ·

3 stems spray orchid

· · ·

4 glory lily heads

· · ·

10 Scarborough lily flowers

· · ·

6 small different coloured ceramic containers

· · ·

scissors

Sometimes we are left with flowers on stems which are too short for large arrangements. Perhaps they are flowers salvaged from fading displays which have been cut shorter to extend their lives or perhaps they are simply broken stems. Nevertheless, they can still be used to good effect.

1 Consider the shape, size, colour and texture of the materials and containers to decide which flowers are appropriate to which container. Also decide whether to use a single flowerhead, or a group display for each container.

2 Measure the flower stem lengths against their container. Anthurium is a single display, as is the pineapple but with willow and exotic leaves. The celosia, orchids, glory lily and Scarborough lily are all used to create a massed effect.

ALL-FOLIAGE ARRANGEMENT

· · ·

MATERIALS

· · ·

2 blocks plastic foam

· · ·

shallow bowl large enough for the plastic foam blocks

· · ·

florist's adhesive tape

· · ·

scissors

· · ·

.71 wires

· · ·

bun moss

· · ·

5 stems grevillea

· · ·

10 stems shrimp plant (Beloperone guttata)

· · ·

10 stems ming fern (cultivar of Boston fern)

· · ·

10 stems pittosporum

· · ·

5 stems cotoneaster

Do not restrict yourself to green foliage; remember the bright yellow of elaeagnus, the silver grey of senecio, not to mention the extraordinary autumn wealth of coloured berries and leaves – all can be used to achieve truly wonderful results.

If the garden is void of flowers, your budget is limited, or you simply fancy a change, then creating an arrangement entirely from different types of foliage can be both challenging and rewarding.

No matter what the season, finding three or four varieties of foliage is not difficult. Anything from the common privet to the most exotic shrubs can be used and to great effect.

1 Soak the plastic foam and secure it in the bowl with florist's adhesive tape.

2 Make hairpin shapes from .71 wire and pin clumps of bun moss around the rim of the bowl by pushing the wires through the moss into the plastic foam. This conceals the plastic foam where it meets the edge of the bowl.

3 Start arranging the grevillea from one side, to establish the maximum height, and work diagonally across with progressively shorter stems, finishing with foliage flowing over the front of the bowl. Arrange the shrimp plant in a similar way along the opposite diagonal, but make it shorter than the grevillea and emphasize this line by adding ming fern.

4 Strengthen the line of grevillea by interspersing it with the broader-leafed pittosporum. Finally, distribute the cotoneaster evenly throughout the whole arrangement.

GERBERA BOTTLE DISPLAY

· · ·

MATERIALS

· · ·

red food colouring

· · ·

yellow food colouring

· · ·

*pitcher, for mixing food
colourings*

· · ·

6 bottles or tall, slim vases

· · ·

12 gerberas in various colours

· · ·

scissors

*Gerberas have soft flexible
stems which tend to bend
naturally. To straighten them,
wrap together the top three
quarters of their stems in paper
to keep them erect. Then stand
them in deep cool water for
approximately two hours.*

The success of a display of flowers need not rely on its complexity; indeed it is held by many that simplicity is the essence of good design.

The flowers of the gerbera have an extraordinary visual innocence and a vast array of vibrant colours. This powerful graphic quality makes the gerbera perfect for simple, bold, modern designs which this arrangement demonstrates by isolating blooms in separate containers within an overall grouping. The impact is perpetuated in the water by the addition of food colouring.

1 Add the red and yellow food colourings separately to water and mix thoroughly together. Fill the various bottles or vases. For maximum impact, choose different shapes and sizes of bottles and vary the strength of food colouring to each vessel. The food colouring will not harm the flowers in any way.

2 Measure the gerbera stems to the desired height and cut them at an angle. Place them in bottles individually or in twos and threes, depending on the size of the bottle neck. Finally, arrange the bottles in an eye-catching group, using other colourful props if desired.

GROWING PLANTS TABLE DECORATION

• • •

It is possible to avoid the time-consuming preparation which is a necessary part of flower arranging by using potted plants. A table decoration need not be the traditional arrangement of cut flowers. An interesting selection of contrasting small plants of different heights has been used in this display. Their status has been elevated by planting them in old terracotta pots of different sizes to give variation to the height of the decoration.

To tie the display together visually, the pots are grouped with interspersed coloured night-lights (tea-lights), each sitting on a leaf which is not only decorative, but will also catch the dripping wax.

MATERIALS
• • •
2 violas
• • •
2 ornamental cabbages
• • •
1 African violet
• • •
1 cyclamen
• • •
6 small terracotta pots of different sizes
• • •
bun moss
• • •
night-lights (tea-lights)
• • •
large leaves

1 Remove all the plants from their plastic containers, plant them in terracotta pots, and then water well. Cover the top of the soil in the pots with fresh, moist bun moss. Be sure to allow the pots to drain thoroughly. Arrange the pots at the centre of the table and intersperse with night-lights (tea-lights) placed on leaves, large enough to be visible and to catch the dripping wax.

The group can be as large or small as the table size dictates and the plants can be used around the house between dinner parties.
Never leave burning candles unattended and do not allow them to burn down to within 5cm (2in) of the display.

APRICOT ROSE AND PUMPKIN

$\cdot \cdot \cdot$

MATERIALS

$\cdot \cdot \cdot$

1 block plastic foam

$\cdot \cdot \cdot$

knife

$\cdot \cdot \cdot$

*marble bird bath, or similar
container*

$\cdot \cdot \cdot$

florist's adhesive tape

$\cdot \cdot \cdot$

scissors

$\cdot \cdot \cdot$

10 stems hypericum

$\cdot \cdot \cdot$

5 tiny pumpkins

$\cdot \cdot \cdot$

.71 wires

$\cdot \cdot \cdot$

10 stems apricot spray roses

The simple appeal of this design results from its use of just one type of flower and one type of foliage. The addition of tiny pumpkins gives body to the pretty combination of spray roses and flowering hypericum foliage. Note how the apricot colour is carried through the flowers, pumpkins and container in contrast to the red buds and yellow flowers of the foliage.

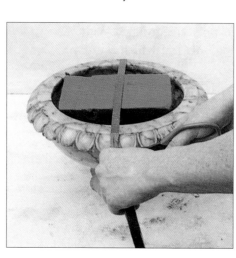

1 Soak the block of plastic foam and cut it so that it can be wedged in place in the container. Secure the foam with florist's adhesive tape.

2 Create the outline of the display using the hypericum and establish its overall height, width and length. The stems of commercially-produced hypericum tend to be long and straight with many offshoots of smaller stems. To create a more delicate foliage effect, and to get the most out of your material, use these smaller stems in the arrangement.

3 Wire each pumpkin by pushing one wire right through across the pumpkin base and out of the other side. Push another wire through to cross the first at right angles. Pull both wires down so that they project from the base. The pumpkins will be supported by pushing these wires into the plastic foam.

4 Position the pumpkins in the foliage, making sure that some are recessed more than others.

5 Infill the arrangement with the spray roses. Like the hypericum, spray roses tend to have lots of small offshoots from the main stem and these should be used to get the most out of your materials. To augment the overall shape of the display, use buds on longer stems at the outside edges with the most open blooms and heavily-flowered stems in the centre.

Substituting limes for the pumpkins will add a touch of vibrancy but for a more sophisticated look, use plums or black grapes.

53

EXOTIC NAPKIN DECORATION
· · ·

MATERIALS

· · ·

napkin

· · ·

trails (sprays) passion flower

· · ·

scissors

· · ·

2-3 virginia creeper leaves

· · ·

1 glory lily head

· · ·

1 celosia head

Exotic flowers are surprisingly robust, so you can prepare the napkin decorations in advance of your dinner party and they will not droop.

When Oriental food is on the menu, this easy-to-make napkin decoration will give the dining table the perfect finishing touch.

Passion flower trails (sprays) are bound around the napkin and tied off in a knot into which the flowerheads and leaves are pushed to hold them in place.

1 Fold the napkin into a rectangle and then loosely roll up. Wrap a passion flower trail (spray) around its middle, pulling quite tightly but taking care not to snap it, then tie off in a simple knot.

2 Using the virginia creeper leaves, start arranging the decoration on the napkin by carefully pushing the stems through the knot, then repeat the process with the flowerheads.

HERBAL TABLE DECORATION
. . .

This table decoration is made up of five elements: four terracotta pots of various herbs, foliages contained within a plastic foam ring, night-lights (tea-lights) and white dill. This is an interesting alternative to the more conventional concept of an arrangement held in plastic foam, or wire mesh, in a single container.

MATERIALS
. . .
6 night-lights (tea-lights)
. . .
30 cm (12 in) diameter plastic foam wreath frame
. . .
2 blocks plastic foam
. . .
4 terracotta pots
. . .
cellophane (plastic wrap)
. . .
scissors
. . .
white dill
. . .
rosemary
. . .
mint
. . .
marjoram
. . .
guelder rose
(Viburnum opulus)
(European cranberry) berries

This display can be dismantled and the parts used separately to good effect in different situations. The individual terracotta pots of herbs can even be dried and their usefulness extended. Never leave burning candles unattended.

1 Press the night-lights (tea-lights) into the soaked plastic foam ring, at equal distances around its circumference. Soak the block of plastic foam and line the terracotta pots with cellophane to prevent leakage. Cut the plastic foam to size and fit it firmly into the pots.

2 Mass the white dill around the base ring between the night-lights (tea-lights). Then mass the individual pots with selected herbs and foliage. The effect is greater if each pot is filled with one type of herb only. Position the base ring and arrange the pots within it.

TABLE ARRANGEMENT WITH FRUIT AND FLOWERS

· · ·

MATERIALS

· · ·

basket

· · ·

cellophane (plastic wrap)

· · ·

2 blocks plastic foam

· · ·

scissors

· · ·

florist's adhesive tape

· · ·

1 bundle tree ivy

· · ·

3 bunches red grapes

· · ·

.71 wires

· · ·

6 black figs

· · ·

15 stems antirrhinum

· · ·

15 stems amaranthus (straight, not trailing)

· · ·

15 stems astilbe

· · ·

20 stems red roses

· · ·

5 stems hydrangea

The addition of fruit brings a visual opulence to this arrangement of flowers. The sumptuous reds and purples of the figs and grapes used in this display harmonize beautifully with the rich deep hues of the flowers. The natural bloom on the fruit combines with the velvet softness of the roses to create a textural feast for the eye. The overall effect is one of ravishing lusciousness.

1 Line the basket with cellophane (plastic wrap) and tightly wedge in the blocks of water-soaked plastic foam. Trim the excess cellophane around the edge of the basket. If the arrangement is to be moved, tape the foam firmly in place.

2 To establish the overall shape of the arrangement, create a low dome of foliage with the tree ivy in proportion with the size and shape of the basket. Spread the tree ivy evenly throughout the plastic foam.

3 Wire the bunches of grapes by double leg mounting on .71 wires. Position the bunches recessed in the foliage in a roughly diagonal line across the display. Handle the grapes delicately.

4 Push a wire through each fig from side to side, leaving projecting ends to bend downwards. Group the figs in pairs and push the wires into the plastic foam around the centre of the arrangement.

5 Emphasize the domed shape of the display with the antirrhinums, amaranthus and the astilbe. Then add the roses, which are the focal flowers, evenly through the display. To complete the arrangement, recess the hydrangea heads into the plastic foam to give depth and texture. Water the foam daily to prolong the life of the display.

Although there are numerous ingredients in this display, the final effect is well worth the extra attention.

OLD-FASHIONED GARDEN ROSE ARRANGEMENT

· · ·

MATERIALS

· · ·

watertight container, to put inside plant pot

· · ·

low, weathered terracotta plant pot

· · ·

pitcher

· · ·

variety garden roses, short- and long-stemmed

· · ·

scissors

The technique is to mass one type of flower in several varieties whose papery petals will achieve a textural mix of colour and scent.

The beautiful full-blown blooms of these antique-looking roses give an opulent and romantic feel to a very simple combination of flower and container. This arrangement deserves centre stage in any room setting.

1 Place the watertight container inside the terracotta plant pot and fill with water. Fill the pitcher as well. Select and prepare your blooms and remove the lower foliage and thorns.

2 Position the longer-stemmed blooms in the pitcher with the heads massed together. This ensures that the cut stems are supported and so can simply be placed directly into the water.

3 Mass shorter, more open flowerheads in the glass bowl inside the plant pot with the stems hidden and the heads showing just above the rim of the pot. The heads look best if kept either all on one level or in a slight dome shape. If fewer flowers are used, wire mesh or plastic foam may be needed to control the positions of individual blooms.

BLUE AND YELLOW BUD VASES
• • •

MATERIALS

• • •

2 bud vases

• • •

3 stems helenium

• • •

scissors

• • •

5 virginia creeper leaves

• • •

3 stems delphinium

• • •

2 stems campanula

• • •

3 small vine leaves

• • •

raffia

When deciding on a bud vase and its contents, consider both the size of the table and the proportion of flowers to the container used. Generally bud vases are used on small dining tables and therefore must not be too large and obtrusive. Also a small container with tall flowers is unstable and likely to be knocked over. The water should be changed, or at least topped-up, daily.

The bud vase is possibly the most common form of table decoration, but that does not mean that it has to be commonplace. These delightful examples, using primary colours, demonstrate that with just a little imagination the simple bud vase can be exciting.

1 Fill the vases approximately three-quarters full with water. Measure the stems of your helenium next to your chosen vase in order to achieve the correct height, then cut the stems at an angle and place in the vase. Position virginia creeper leaves around the top of the vase to frame the helenium.

2 Use two or three flowered stems of delphinium and also use the delicate tendrils of buds which are perfect for small arrangements. Prune the relatively large leaves of the campanula before adding. Finally, position the vine leaves around the base of the flowers in the neck of the vase, and finish off each vase with a raffia tie.

SUMMER BASKET DISPLAY

· · ·

Summer brings an abundance of varied and beautiful material for the flower arranger. The lovely scents, luscious blooms and vast range of colours available provide endless possibilities for creating wonderful displays.

This arrangement is a bountiful basket, overflowing with seasonal summer blooms which is designed for a large table or sideboard but could be scaled up or down to suit any situation.

MATERIALS
· · ·
basket
· · ·
cellophane (plastic wrap)
· · ·
scissors
· · ·
2 blocks plastic foam
· · ·
florist's adhesive tape
· · ·
10 stems Viburnum tinus
· · ·
15 stems larkspur in 3 colours
· · ·
6 lily stems, such as 'Stargazer'
· · ·
5 large ivy leaves
· · ·
10 stems white phlox

Keep the display well watered and it should go on flowering for at least a week. The lilies should open fully in plastic foam and new phlox buds will keep opening to replace the spent heads.

1 Line the basket with cellophane (plastic wrap) to prevent leakage, and cut to fit. Then secure the two soaked blocks of plastic foam in the lined basket with the florist's adhesive tape.

2 Arrange the viburnum stems in the plastic foam to establish the overall height, width and shape. Strengthen the outline using the larkspur, making sure you use all of the stems and not just the flower spikes.

3 Place the lilies in a diagonal line across the arrangement. Position the large ivy leaves around the lilies in the centre of the display. Arrange the phlox across the arrangement along the opposite diagonal to the lilies.

61

EXOTIC TABLE ARRANGEMENT

$\bullet \bullet \bullet$

MATERIALS

$\bullet \bullet \bullet$

wire mesh

$\bullet \bullet \bullet$

bowl

$\bullet \bullet \bullet$

10 croton (Codiaeum) leaves

$\bullet \bullet \bullet$

10 red Scarborough lily flowers

$\bullet \bullet \bullet$

5 cockscomb

$\bullet \bullet \bullet$

7 celosia heads

$\bullet \bullet \bullet$

7 glory lilies

$\bullet \bullet \bullet$

.71 wires

$\bullet \bullet \bullet$

1 mango

When planning a table arrangement, choose the container with care. If the container is too large it may obstruct your guests' view across the dinner table.

This feast of red flowers and coloured foliage with its touches of yellow and green is bursting with exotic vibrance. The tiny flame-like petals of the glory lily set against the velvet texture of the celosia create a rich display of light and shade, and the bright yellow ceramic container heightens the overall impact. Use it as a focal point for an extravagant party table.

1 Scrunch up the wire mesh and place it in the bottom of the bowl. Fill approximately two-thirds with water. Position the croton leaves by pushing the stems of leaves into the wire mesh for support, creating a framework within which to build the arrangement.

2 Distribute the Scarborough lily flowers throughout the arrangement by pushing the stems into the wire mesh.

3 Cut the cockscomb to between 15 and 20 cm (6 and 8 in) long and ensure that all foliage is removed as this will rot in the water. Distribute evenly throughout the arrangement pushing the stems into the wire mesh.

4 Cut the glory lily flowers to between 15 and 20 cm (6 and 8 in) and push into the arrangement and through the wire mesh. Ensure you have an even spread of flowerheads throughout the arrangement.

5 Push .71 wires in pairs into the bottom of the mango and cut to between 15 and 20 cm (6 and 8 in). Carefully position the mango off-centre and slightly recessed in the arrangement by pushing the wires through into the wire mesh. Gently part the flowerheads to position the mango to ensure no flowers are damaged in the process. Finally, ensure all stems are in water.

Take care when handling the mango to avoid bruising its delicate skin.

TULIP TOPIARY TREE

· · ·

The flowers used to make this stunning decorative tree are unlike conventional tulips which have only one layer of petals. These tulips have layer upon layer of different sized petals which together create a very dense, rounded head, reminiscent of a peony.

MATERIALS

· · ·

1 block plastic foam for dried flowers

· · ·

knife

· · ·

basket

· · ·

raffia

· · ·

5 30 cm (12 in) cinnamon sticks

· · ·

scissors

· · ·

glue gun and glue

· · ·

.71 wires

· · ·

reindeer moss

· · ·

1 plastic foam ball, approximately 15 cm (6 in) diameter

· · ·

open tulip heads

To get the best result from the flowerheads, they have been spread open to reveal their centres. This not only serves to increase their visual impact but also, of course, increases their surface area which means fewer blooms are needed.

1 Cut and fit the block of dry plastic foam into the basket base. Depending on its stability, the container may need to be weighted with wet sand, stones, or plaster of Paris, for example. Using the raffia, tie the cinnamon sticks together at both top and bottom and push the resulting tree trunk into the foam to approximately 4 cm (1½ in), securing with glue.

2 Make hairpins out of the .71 wires and with these pin the reindeer moss into the plastic foam in the basket at the base of the tree, completely covering the dry plastic foam.

3 Soak the plastic foam ball in cold water. Carefully apply a small amount of hot glue to the top end of the cinnamon stick trunk and push the wet foam ball approximately 4 cm (1½ in) on to it.

4 Make sure that the flowerheads are as open as possible by holding the flower in your hand and gently spreading the petals back, even to the extent of folding those at the edge completely inside-out.

5 Cut the tulip heads with a stem length of approximately 4 cm (1½ in) and push them into the soaked foam ball, covering the surface evenly. Handle the flowerheads with care to avoid crushing.

64

LILY AND HYACINTH PLANTED BASKET

• • •

MATERIALS

• • •

large wire basket

• • •

bun or carpet moss

• • •

cellophane (plastic wrap)

• • •

scissors

• • •

3 flowering lily plants (3 stems per pot), such as 'Mona Lisa'

• • •

3 flowering hyacinth bulbs

• • •

8 red-barked dogwood (Cornus alba) branches (or similar)

• • •

raffia

The branches of red-barked dogwood are tied with raffia to form a decorative and supportive structure around the arrangement. A more formal look can be achieved by substituting bamboo canes, tied perhaps with strips of velvet in rich colours.

When the budget is tight, an economic way of creating a large display with lots of impact is to use plants instead of cut flowers.

This arrangement in a basket combines two totally different plants, which will continue to flower for weeks. The lily buds will open in sequence and their scent, mixed with that of hyacinths, will fill the air with an intoxicating perfume.

1 Line the whole basket with a layer of moss, then in turn line the moss with cellophane (plastic wrap) to contain the moisture. Cut to fit.

2 Using the soil from their pots, plant the three lilies into the lined basket, with the hyacinth bulbs between them. Cover the soil with moss.

3 Push four branches of dogwood through the moss and into the soil to form a square around the plants. Cross those horizontally with four more branches, tying them together with raffia to create a frame, then trim the raffia.

WHITE JAPANESE
ANEMONE VASE
• • •

This delightful arrangement combining forest fruits and rosehips with garden anemones, though simple in concept, becomes a sumptuous display when placed in this elegant vase.

MATERIALS
• • •
vase
• • •
scissors
• • •
*blackberries still on
their stems*
• • •
rosehips on stems
• • •
*white Japanese anemones
'Honorine Jobert'*
• • •
vine leaves

The simplest things can be the most effective but when arranging flowers in water, without the help of plastic foam or wire mesh, it is important to consider very carefully the visual effect of the container on the flowers. The rosehips and blackberry stalks used here are very prickly; they need careful handling and the thorns need to be stripped. However, these stems form a strong framework to hold the delicate anemones in position. The addition of vine leaves around the neck of the vase provides a finishing touch for the arrangement.

1 Having filled the vase with water, use the blackberry stems to establish the outline shape. Add the stems of rosehips to reinforce both the structure and the visual balance of the display.

2 Add the anemones evenly throughout the arrangement. Take great care with anemones as they are extremely delicate.

3 Place the stems of the vine leaves in the water so that they form a collar around the base of the arrangement and are visible above the neck of the vase.

Hydrangea Basket Edging

MATERIALS

· · ·

30 autumn leaves

· · ·

.71 wires

· · ·

scissors

· · ·

30 fresh late hydrangea heads

· · ·

basket

· · ·

.32 silver reel (rose) wire

Hydrangea heads cut late in their growing season have toughened and will not wilt out of water. These together with autumn leaves, selected so that they are pliable enough to wire, have been used in a floral decoration which can evolve from fresh to dry and remain attractive.

Take mature hydrangea heads and some autumn leaves, and with a little imagination an old wicker basket is transformed into a delightful container. Whether you fill it with fruit or seasonal pot pourri, this basket will make a decorative and long-lasting addition to your home.

1 Wire the leaves by stitching and double leg mounting on .71 wires.

2 Wire clusters of hydrangea by double leg mounting on .71 wires.

3 Secure the wired hydrangea clusters and leaves alternately around the basket edge by stitching through the gaps in the basket with .32 silver reel (rose) wire. Keep the clusters tightly together to ensure a full edging.

4 When the entire basket edge is covered, finish by stitching the .32 reel wire through several times. If the arrangement is placed in an airy position, the hydrangea heads will dry naturally and prolong the basket's use.

ORNAMENTAL CABBAGE TREE
· · ·

MATERIALS
· · ·
medium-sized terracotta pot
· · ·
cellophane (plastic wrap)
· · ·
sand
· · ·
*1 block plastic foam, for
dried flowers*
· · ·
knife
· · ·
scissors
· · ·
piece of tree root
· · ·
*2 large handfuls sphagnum
moss*
· · ·
twine
· · ·
.71 wires
· · ·
*10 miniature ornamental
cabbages*

*The tree "trunk" is simply a
piece of root, at the top of
which is fixed a moisture-
retaining ball of sphagnum
moss. The cabbage heads are
wired to the moss ball and, by
absorbing water from it and an
occasional mist spraying, will
survive for a week or more.*

Ornamental trees can be created from all sorts of materials for all sorts of decorative uses. This design might be thought unusual in that it uses cabbage
heads to form a "topiary foliage" crown to the tree.

1 Line the medium-sized terracotta pot
with cellophane (plastic wrap) and
approximately half fill with wet sand for
stability. Cut a piece of plastic foam and
wedge it into the pot on top of the sand.
Trim the cellophane if necessary.

2 Push the root into the plastic foam.
Make sure you do this only once as
repeated adjustments will loosen the grip
of the foam and the "trunk" will not be
stable. (Indeed, you could help make it
more secure by placing some glue on the
root base before pushing it into the foam.)
Form a generous handful of sphagnum
moss into a dense ball by criss-crossing it
around with twine.

3 Push the moss ball on to the top of
the root and secure it by threading
wires horizontally through it, leaving the
projecting ends to pull down and wrap
around the "trunk".

4 Using .71 wires, double leg mount the
miniature ornamental cabbage heads
and individually stitch wire any loose
cabbage leaves.

5 Push the wires projecting from the cabbage heads into the moss ball to cover it completely. Fill any gaps with the individual leaves.

6 Make hairpin shapes from .71 wires to fix sphagnum moss to the plastic foam at the base of the tree making sure it is completely covered.

SUNFLOWER PINHOLDER DISPLAY

• • •

MATERIALS

• • •

low ceramic dish

• • •

pinholder

• • •

scissors

• • •

3-5 stems contorted hazel twigs

• • •

9 stems sunflowers

• • •

5 large ivy leaves

The pinholder enables the flower arranger to create beautiful and simple designs without the need for a large container.

The pinholder is weighted so that even the top-heavy sunflowers in this arrangement are totally stable once their stems are pushed onto the metal pins.

This pinholder display results in an informal and minimalist grouping whose glorious sunflowers, set against a backdrop of contorted hazel, shine out undiminished by the clutter of other flowers.

1 Fill the dish with sufficient water to cover the pinholder. Cut the stems of hazel and push them on to the pins to create a tall outline shape.

2 Position the sunflowers, pushing the cut stems on to the pins. Grade the flowers according to the size of their heads. The smallest heads should be on the tallest stems at the top of the arrangement, with the larger heads on shorter stems towards the focal point. Create a staggered line of blooms from top to bottom. Recess a couple of flowerheads and bring the line of flowers over the front of the container to one side, following the outline formed by the contorted hazel.

3 Position the ivy leaves around the focal flower at the centre and add others low down in the display. The leaves will help give visual depth and their dark, green colour will be a suitable background for the bright yellow of the flowers.

Yellow Calla Lily Arrangement
· · ·

This display highlights the striking beauty of the calla lily. It ingeniously exploits the visual power of the almost luminescent golden-yellow blooms of this flower by setting them against a carefully controlled background of blue and green accompanying material.

The chincherinchees have cool green stems and creamy white flowerheads with beady black centres which give interest as well as height to the arrangement.

The viburnum is used as a framework for the display and its metallic blue berries provide a visual bridge between the two flowers it accompanies.

MATERIALS
· · ·
shallow dish
· · ·
pinholder
· · ·
scissors
· · ·
10 stems viburnum berries
· · ·
11 stems Moroccan chincherinchee (Ornithogalum arabicum)
· · ·
5 stems yellow calla lily

The whole arrangement is mounted on a pinholder which becomes almost invisible, so avoiding the distraction of a container.

1 Fill the shallow dish with sufficient water to cover the pinholder when placed within it. Arrange the viburnum by pushing the cut stem ends down onto the pins and use this foliage to create the outline shape of the display and establish its height and width.

2 Arrange the chincherinchees on the pins to run diagonally through the viburnum foliage outline, varying the stem heights.

3 Arrange the calla lilies on the pins. Roughly follow an "S" shape, with the smallest bloom on the longest stem at the back, working forwards and down with larger blooms on shorter stems.

AUTUMN CROCUS TRUG

· · ·

MATERIALS

· · ·

trug

· · ·

cellophane (plastic wrap)

· · ·

6 flowering crocus bulbs

· · ·

bun moss

· · ·

autumn leaves

· · ·

raffia

· · ·

scissors

Although one expects to see crocuses in the spring, this beautiful autumn variety is a welcome sight as its flowers push up determinedly through the fallen leaves. Of course, they do not have to be confined to the garden.

Bring the outdoors inside by planting up an old trug with flowering crocus bulbs in soil covered in a natural-looking carpet of moss and leaves. This simple display is as effective as the most sophisticated cut-flower arrangement.

1 Line the trug with cellophane (plastic wrap) and plant the bulbs in soil.

2 Ensure the bulbs are firmly planted and watered. Arrange the bun moss on top of the soil, then scatter the leaves over the moss to create an autumnal effect.

3 Tie raffia into bows, one on either side of the base of the trug handle.

AUTUMN CANDLE DISPLAY

· · ·

MATERIALS

· · ·

1 block plastic foam

· · ·

1 metal candleholder

· · ·

6 crab apples

· · ·

1 small pumpkin

· · ·

*3 Chinese lantern
heads*

· · ·

.71 wires, .38 wires

· · ·

scissors

· · ·

hypericum buds

· · ·

2 stems spray roses

· · ·

1 beeswax candle

*Beeswax candles have an
attractive texture and natural
honey colouring which are the
perfect accompaniment for this
seasonal rustic display.*

The autumn fruits of Chinese lanterns, crab apples and baby pumpkins are put to good use in this charming and compact candle decoration. The natural rich colouring of the fruits and the deep red of the hypericum buds complement beautifully the soft apricot tones of the spray roses.

1 Soak the plastic foam in water and cut it into small pieces to fit into the candleholder drip tray. Firmly wedge into the drip tray to support the arrangement.

2 Wire the crab apples and pumpkin on .71 wires and Chinese lantern heads on .38 wires. All wires should be cut to approximately 4 cm (1½ in) in length.

3 By pushing wires into the foam, position the pumpkin, 2 groups of 3 crab apples and a group of 3 Chinese lantern heads, spacing them equally around the circumference of the drip tray.

4 Arrange the hypericum foliage between the fruits by pushing short stems into the plastic foam to create the outline shape of the display.

5 Cut flowerheads from the spray roses on stems long enough to push into the plastic foam amongst the foliage and fruits. Use rose buds towards the outside edge of the arrangement, and more open blooms towards the centre. Remember to ensure that there is enough space left to accommodate the beeswax candle.

Never leave burning candles unattended and do not allow them to burn down to within 5 cm (2 in) of the display height.

BLUE AND YELLOW ARRANGEMENT IN A PITCHER

• • •

MATERIALS

• • •

10 stems 'Blue Butterfly' delphinium

• • •

2 bunches sneezeweed (Helenium)

• • •

3 stems dracaena

• • •

raffia

• • •

scissors

• • •

pitcher

The choice of container is important since it becomes a major element in the design. The yellow pitcher gives the display a country look, but of course the same arrangement would look more sophisticated if the container was a contemporary glass vase.

The sunny yellow faces of sneezeweed become almost luminous when set against the electric blue colour of 'Blue Butterfly' delphinium, a brave colour combination guaranteed to brighten any situation. The easy-to-make, hand-tied spiral bunch is designed to look as though the flowers have just been cut and loosely arranged.

1 Lay out the materials for ease of working. Build the display by alternately adding stems of different material while continuously turning the growing bunch in your hand so that the stems form a spiral.

2 Continue the process until all materials are used and you have a full display of flowers. At the binding point, i.e. where all the stems cross, tie firmly with raffia. Trim the stem ends to the length dictated by the container.

LARGE DAHLIA ARRANGEMENT

· · ·

Dahlias bloom vigorously all through the summer and until the first frosts of autumn, offering dazzling variations of colour and shape for the flower arranger. The complex and precise geometry of the dahlia flowerheads ensures that, even with the informality of the bright red rosehips and softness of the campanulas, the arrangement retains a structured feel.

MATERIALS
· · ·
large, watertight pot
· · ·
15 stems campanula
· · ·
scissors
· · ·
10 stems long-stemmed rosehips
· · ·
30 stems pompom dahlias

These beautiful golden dahlias have clean, long straight stems which makes them easy to arrange in a large display. They would also survive well in plastic foam.

1 Fill the pot three-quarters full with water. Create the basic domed outline and the structure using the leafy campanula.

2 Cut and strip the thorns from the stems of the rosehips and arrange in amongst the campanula, varying the heights as required to follow the domed outline.

3 Cut the pompom dahlias to the required heights and add to the arrangement, distributing them evenly throughout. The aim is to achieve a smooth domed effect.

MANTELPIECE ARRANGEMENT

· · ·

MATERIALS

· · ·

1 block plastic foam

· · ·

plastic tray for plastic foam

· · ·

florist's adhesive tape

· · ·

scissors

· · ·

5 stems birch twigs

· · ·

*6 stems Butcher's broom
(Ruscus)*

· · ·

*5 stems Eupohorbia
fulgens*

· · ·

7 stems straight amaranthus

· · ·

5 stems spray chrysanthemums

· · ·

5 stems alstroemeria

· · ·

7 stems eustoma

*On its own, or combined with
a fireplace arrangement
(pictured opposite and featured
over the page), this mantelpiece
arrangement creates a stunning
focal point to a room.*

The mantelpiece offers a prominent position for a floral display. The challenge is to create not just a visual balance, but a physical balance too. The mantel shelf is relatively narrow and flowers must be carefully positioned to avoid them toppling forwards. So, as you build, ensure stability by keeping the weight at the back and as near the bottom of the display as is practical.

The delicate stems of ruscus and euphorbia fulgens are lightweight in relation to their length and thus ideal for this type of arrangement. Their natural trailing habit means they can be positioned to give width along the shelf and length over its front edge and, together with birch twigs, they give the display its structure. The addition of a selection of strongly coloured flowers brings the arrangement vibrantly alive.

1 Soak the block of plastic foam in cold water and securely tape into the plastic tray with florist's adhesive tape. Position the tray at the centre of the mantelpiece.

2 Arrange the birch twigs and ruscus in the plastic foam to establish height and width. Take advantage of the natural curving habit of the ruscus to trail over the container.

3 Add the scarlet plume to emphasize the trailing nature of the display. Distribute the amaranthus throughout the display to reinforce the established shape.

4 The spray chrysanthemums are the focal flowers and should be roughly staggered to either side of the vertical axis at the centre of the display. The alstroemeria stems add strength and, by recessing one or two of them, depth to the arrangement.

5 A stem of good quality eustoma has two to three side stems. Split these off to make the most of the flowers. Use budded stems towards the outside of the display and more open blooms towards its centre, making sure some are recessed to give visual depth.

FIREPLACE ARRANGEMENT

. . .

MATERIALS

. . .

2 blocks plastic foam

. . .

1 plastic-lined basket

. . .

florist's adhesive tape

. . .

scissors

. . .

*10 stems Butcher's broom
(ruscus)*

. . .

6 stems birch twigs

. . .

*10 stems Euphorbia
fulgens*

. . .

5 stems orange lilies

. . .

5 stems red alstroemeria

. . .

*5 stems spray
chrysanthemums*

. . .

10 stems orange tulips

. . .

10 stems eustoma

A fireplace is the focal point of a room, but without a fire, an empty grate can be an eyesore. Turn this to your advantage by filling the hearth with an arrangement of flowers.

In the absence of real flames, this display substitutes the bright, fiery reds, oranges and yellows of scarlet plume, alstroemeria, tulips, lilies and chrysanthemums. This colour palette is given depth and richness by the purple of eustoma. The languid forms of ruscus, with the stark outlines of birch twigs, define the architecture of the arrangement.

1 Soak the plastic foam in water and secure in the basket using florist's adhesive tape. Place the basket in the grate of the fireplace.

2 Arrange the ruscus and the birch twigs to create a foliage outline, taking advantage of the natural curves of the ruscus to achieve a flowing effect.

3 Use the scarlet plume to reinforce the outline and define the height of the display. The lilies are the focal flowers and should be arranged to follow roughly a diagonal through the display. The alstroemeria should be positioned to follow the opposite diagonal. Decrease the length of the stems of both flowers from the rear to the front.

4 Arrange the spray chrysanthemums, approximately following, and thus reinforcing, the line of lilies. Again reduce the chrysanthemum stem height from rear to front. Finally, distribute the tulips and eustoma evenly through the arrangement using the most open of the eustoma blooms towards the centre.

ARUM LILY VASE

· · ·

Pure in colour and form, elegant and stately, the arum lily has the presence to be displayed on its own, supported by the minimum of well-chosen foliage. Here it is arranged with the wonderfully curious contorted willow and the large, simple leaves of aucuba. Because they do not compete visually, the willow and the aucuba serve purely as a backdrop to the beauty of the arum.

MATERIALS

· · ·

vase

· · ·

scissors

· · ·

branches of contorted willow

· · ·

6 arum lilies

· · ·

2 bushy branches aucuba 'Gold Dust'

The choice of container is of great importance, the visual requirement being for simple unfussy shapes, with glass and metal being particularly appropriate. The chosen vase should complement the sculptural impact of the arum.

1 Fill the vase to approximately three-quarters with water. Arrange the contorted willow in the vase to establish the overall height of the arrangement. (When cutting a willow stem to the right length, cut the base at a 45° angle and scrape the bark off to approximately 5 cm (2 in) from the end, then split this section.)

2 Arrange the arum lilies at different heights throughout the willow to achieve a visual balance. The willow stems will help support the blooms.

3 Give visual substance to the display by adding stems of aucuba throughout to provide a dark backdrop to throw the arum blooms into sharp relief.

CANDELABRA TABLE DECORATION

• • •

MATERIALS

• • •

candelabra

• • •

plastic foam ring,
30 cm (12 in) in diameter

• • •

scissors

• • •

20 short stems Viburnum
tinus, *in flower*

• • •

20 short stems variegated
pieris

• • •

15 heads Easter lily

• • •

10 stems purple aster

• • •

3 trails (sprigs) variegated ivy

Never leave burning candles
unattended and do not allow
them to burn down to within
less than 5 cm (2 in) of the
display height.

The classic combination of flowers and candlelight is usually associated with romantic dinners for two. However, this candelabra table decoration is appropriate to a variety of special dining occasions. Stately candles floating on a sumptuous sea of white lilies and purple asters make a decoration suitable for even the most formal of events.

1 Soak the plastic foam ring in cold water and position the candelabra within the ring. As the arrangement will eventually involve ivy being attached to both the candelabra and ring, it is advisable to create this display *in situ*. Using approximately 10 cm (4 in) long stems of viburnum and variegated pieris, push into the foam to create an even foliage outline.

2 Cut the lily heads leaving about 7.5 cm (3 in) of stem to push into the foam. Group the heads in threes around the circumference of the foam ring. Generally the groups should have one open bloom placed towards the centre with two buds at the outside edge of the ring. But in so doing, remember buds will open in 24 hours to fill the areas.

3 Aster flowers usually have a sturdy main stem and several side stems with flowerheads which should be separated. Cut all the aster stems to approximately 10 cm (4 in) lengths, and distribute evenly through the arrangement, pushing firmly into the plastic foam.

4 Ivy will survive out of water for a time but to ensure it remains in good condition for the life of the decoration, push the cut end of the trail (sprig) into the soaked plastic foam before entwining it around the candelabra. For safety reasons, do not allow any ivy leaves to come up over the candleholder's wax guards.

ORANGE ARRANGEMENT

· · ·

MATERIALS

· · ·

wire basket

· · ·

reindeer moss

· · ·

cellophane (plastic wrap)

· · ·

1 block plastic foam

· · ·

knife

· · ·

florist's adhesive tape

· · ·

scissors

· · ·

10 stems salal tips

· · ·

7 stems orange lily

· · ·

10 stems orange tulip

· · ·

20 stems marigold

The matt green of salal tips creates the perfect background for the spectacular zesty orange colour of the three different flowers used in this display. The arrangement is a dome of flowers supported in plastic foam in a wire basket.

1 Line the basket with a layer of reindeer moss, about 3 cm (1½ in) thick, and line the moss with cellophane (plastic wrap). Cut a block of water-soaked plastic foam to fit the basket and tape securely in place.

2 Push the salal tips into the plastic foam to create a dome-shaped foliage outline in proportion with the container. Salal tips have relatively large rounded leaves which generally should be used sparingly to avoid overwhelming the flowers. However, the strength of the colour and shape of the flowers in this particular arrangement works well with the bold salal leaves.

3 Cut the lily stems to a length to suit the foliage framework and push into the foam evenly throughout the arrangement to reinforce the overall shape.

4 Distribute the tulips evenly through the display, remembering they will continue to grow and their natural downward curve will tend to straighten.

5 Add the marigolds last, positioning them evenly throughout the display. Remember the marigold stems are soft, so take care when pushing them into the plastic foam.

There are two points worth remembering. First the tulips will continue to grow and straighten in the plastic foam, so make allowance for this in your dome shape; second, any buds on the lilies will open, so give them the space to do so.

DECORATED VASE WITH CALLA LILIES

· · ·

MATERIALS

· · ·

a selection of lichen-covered twigs

· · ·

glass vase

· · ·

raffia

· · ·

scissors

· · ·

10 red antirrhinums

· · ·

15 calla lilies

· · ·

3 calla lily leaves

By making the twigs project above the top of the vase, they become an integral part of the arrangement and provide helpful support for the flowers. An alternative look could be created by gluing the heads of dried flowers, such as sunflowers, all over a plain glass vase.

A novel and simple way to transform a container is to decorate its outside with organic material. This example uses lichen-covered twigs and is particularly practical since after the arrangement in the vase has died the twigs will have dried out and, with careful handling, can be kept on the vase for the next display.

1 The twigs have to be fixed securely to the vase. To do this, make two lengths of bundles of raffia and lay on these sufficient twigs to go around the circumference of the vase. Place the vase on its side, on the twigs, and tie firmly with the lengths of raffia. Trim the twig stems level with the base of the vase.

2 Stand the vase upright and three-quarter fill with water. Begin with the red antirrhinums, placing them towards the back to establish the height and width of the arrangement's framework.

3 Distribute the calla lily blooms evenly throughout the arrangement, varying their heights to achieve a visual balance and a good profile. Add the calla lily leaves diagonally through the arrangement, reducing their height from the back to the front. This will visually emphasize the depth of the arrangement.

WINTER TWIGS
ARRANGEMENT
· · ·

Cut flowers can be expensive during the winter months but this does not mean flower arranging has to stop. This display is created from the types of winter growth found in domestic gardens. It is simple to arrange and offers a scale suitable to decorate a large space.

Delicate lichen softens the otherwise rough branches of larch while the beautiful and scented winter-flowering viburnum adds a touch of spring. Finally the deep red stems of red-barked dogwood provide a strength of colour which will persist throughout the life of the display and even beyond if dried.

MATERIALS
· · ·
5 stems lichen-covered larch twigs
· · ·
scissors and secateurs
· · ·
large ceramic pot
· · ·
5-10 stems red-barked dogwood
· · ·
10 stems Viburnum x bodnantense 'Dawn'

1 Cut the larch twigs so that the majority are at the maximum height of the display, and arrange to the outline shape. The container should be about one-third of the overall display height.

2 Cut the red-barked dogwood and arrange amongst the larch twigs so that the stems at the rear of the display are at their maximum height, becoming shorter towards the front.

As a general rule when using twigs, remember to strip the stem ends of bark and lichen otherwise they will rot, accelerate the formation of bacteria, shorten the life of the display and very quickly cause the water to smell.

3 Add the flowering viburnum, again varying its length from tall at the rear to shorter at the front. To avoid rotting, be sure to strip off all bark and flowers from the stem ends in the water and split any thick woody stems to allow water in.

HERB OBELISK

・ ・ ・

MATERIALS

・ ・ ・

ruler

・ ・ ・

pencil

・ ・ ・

1 block plastic foam

・ ・ ・

sharp knife

・ ・ ・

suitable container

・ ・ ・

7 radishes

・ ・ ・

8 button mushrooms

・ ・ ・

9 small, clean new potatoes

・ ・ ・

.71 wires

・ ・ ・

scissors

・ ・ ・

dill

・ ・ ・

curry plant

・ ・ ・

marjoram

・ ・ ・

mint

・ ・ ・

bay leaves

The urn container gives the obelisk a grand look, but a less formal, more rustic feel can be achieved by using a terracotta plant pot or mossy basket.

A colourful pillar of herbs and vegetables which looks wonderful on its own and even more striking when used in pairs. It is particularly suitable for a buffet table decoration but can also be used simply as a decorative object in any appropriate setting.

1 Using a ruler and pencil score the cutting lines on the block of plastic foam. Carve the block to the required shape using a sharp knife. Soak the carved plastic foam shape and secure firmly in your chosen container.

3 Fill in the gaps between rings of vegetables, using a different herb for each ring. Finally select a quantity of bay leaves of similar size and insert them into the plastic foam under the bottom layer of vegetables to create a formal border.

Right: Detail of the final arrangement

2 Wire all the vegetables by pushing a .71 wire through from one side to the other, leaving sufficient wire projecting on both sides to allow you to pull down and out of the base to approximately 4 cm (1½ in). Mushrooms are very fragile and particular care must be taken when wiring these. Having decided on the order you want to use the vegetables, work from the bottom of the obelisk upwards, pushing the wires into the plastic foam to position the vegetables in horizontal rings around the shape.

PARROT TULIP CANDLE DECORATION

· · ·

MATERIALS

· · ·

plastic foam ring, 15 cm (6 in) diameter, and holder

· · ·

candle, 7.5 x 22.5 cm (3 x 9 in)

· · ·

scissors

· · ·

approximately 7-8 very open 'Parrot' tulip heads

Other flowers, such as roses and buttercups can, when their flowerheads are full, have their useful lives extended by the use of this technique.
Never leave a burning candle unattended and do not allow it to burn down to within less than 5 cm (2 in) of the display height.

There is a tendency to think that a fully opened bloom is at the end of its useful life. However, these Parrot tulip heads have had their lives extended by the simple process of shortening their stems. The red and yellow of the spreading petals of these tulips create an impression of flames licking up the candle.

1 Soak the plastic foam ring in water and position the candle at its centre. Check that the candle is firmly in position.

2 Cut the tulips to a stem length of approximately 3 cm (1¼ in) and push them into the plastic foam. Repeat this around the entire ring making sure no foam is left exposed.

BERRIED CANDLE
DECORATION
• • •

A commercially-produced red candle in an earthenware pot can be made into a sumptuous table decoration by embellishing it with fruits and foliage from the garden and hedge. This is a technically simple, yet effective, decoration involving sitting the pot in a small wire basket through which the stems of fruit and foliage are artfully woven.

MATERIALS
• • •
candle in an earthenware pot
• • •
small square wire basket, to
accommodate the pot
• • •
Virginia creeper leaves
on stems
• • •
blackberry clusters on stems
• • •
scissors
• • •
rosehip clusters on stems
• • •
.32 silver reel (rose) wire

1 Place the candle pot in the wire basket. Weave Virginia creeper stems through the wire basket around its entire top edge. Then establish a thick garland of Virginia creeper leaves around the basket.

2 For safe handling strip the thorns from the blackberry stems and cut to approximately 6 cm (2 in) long. Push the stems into the Virginia creeper garland and through the wire basket.

The plant materials used are robust enough to survive in good condition for a day or two out of water but would benefit from mist spraying. Never leave burning candles unattended and do not allow them to burn down to within 5 cm (2 in) of the display.

3 Using the same procedure, add the rosehips but in separate small groups around the circumference of the basket. If the decoration is likely to be moved, it is safer to provide additional security for the stems by tying them to the basket with lengths of fine silver reel (rose) wire.

INDEX

. . .

Author Acknowledgements

Fiona Barnett would like to thank Roger Egerickx and Richard Kiss of Design and Display (Sales Ltd) for their generous provision of facilities.
With special thanks to Jenny Bennett for her hard work.